50 Japan Fall Season Recipes for Home

By: Kelly Johnson

Table of Contents

- Kabocha Squash Soup
- Chestnut Rice (Kuri Gohan)
- Sweet Potato Tempura
- Miso Soup with Mushrooms
- Pumpkin Croquettes
- Simmered Daikon Radish
- Japanese Beef Stew
- Autumn Vegetable Stir-Fry
- Grilled Salmon with Teriyaki Sauce
- Roasted Sweet Potatoes with Soy Glaze
- Kinpira Gobo (Braised Burdock Root)
- Soba Noodles with Roasted Pumpkin
- Japanese Pickled Vegetables
- Udon Noodle Soup with Seasonal Veggies
- Sukiyaki
- Japanese Curry Rice with Seasonal Vegetables
- Tempura Pumpkin and Mushrooms
- Sweet Potato and Black Sesame Pudding
- Mushroom Rice (Kinoko Gohan)
- Teriyaki Chicken with Grilled Autumn Vegetables
- Roasted Chestnut Soup
- Sweet Potato and Caramelized Onion Pizza
- Steamed Egg Custard (Chawanmushi)
- Miso Glazed Eggplant
- Japanese Style Beef and Potato Stew
- Apple and Daikon Salad
- Spicy Miso Ramen with Seasonal Vegetables
- Roasted Kabocha and Garlic
- Warm Tofu Salad with Autumn Vegetables
- Nabe Hot Pot with Fall Ingredients
- Japanese Style Sweet Potato Pie
- Roasted Acorn Squash with Miso Butter
- Japanese Pumpkin and Coconut Curry
- Fried Chicken with Apple Slaw
- Grilled Mackerel with Fall Vegetables
- Pickled Sweet Potatoes

- Kabocha and Mushroom Risotto
- Japanese Sweet Potato and Caramel Soup
- Teriyaki Tofu with Stir-Fried Greens
- Spicy Pumpkin Soup with Tofu
- Japanese Salmon and Sweet Potato Bake
- Miso Marinated Pumpkin Salad
- Grilled Eel with Autumn Vegetables
- Sweet Potato and Walnut Rice Balls
- Hot Pot with Kabocha and Tofu
- Udon with Sweet Potato and Spinach
- Japanese Style Squash and Apple Soup
- Roasted Mushroom and Pork Stir-Fry
- Pumpkin and Ginger Muffins
- Soy-Glazed Chicken Wings with Roasted Fall Veggies

Kabocha Squash Soup

Ingredients:

- 1 medium kabocha squash (about 2-3 pounds)
- 1 tablespoon olive oil
- 1 medium onion, diced
- 2 cloves garlic, minced
- 4 cups vegetable or chicken broth
- 1 cup coconut milk (or heavy cream for a richer soup)
- 1 teaspoon grated fresh ginger (optional)
- 1/2 teaspoon ground cumin
- 1/4 teaspoon ground nutmeg
- Salt and pepper to taste
- Fresh cilantro or parsley for garnish (optional)

Instructions:

1. **Prepare the Squash:**
   - Cut the kabocha squash in half and scoop out the seeds. You can roast the seeds for a crunchy snack if you like.
   - Place the squash halves cut side down on a baking sheet and roast at 400°F (200°C) for 40-45 minutes, or until tender. Alternatively, you can peel and cube the squash and steam or boil it until tender.
2. **Make the Soup Base:**
   - Heat olive oil in a large pot over medium heat.
   - Add the diced onion and cook until softened, about 5 minutes.
   - Add the minced garlic and cook for another minute.
3. **Combine Ingredients:**
   - Scoop the roasted squash flesh from the skin and add it to the pot with the onions and garlic.
   - Pour in the vegetable or chicken broth and bring to a boil. Reduce heat and simmer for 10 minutes.
4. **Blend the Soup:**
   - Use an immersion blender to puree the soup directly in the pot until smooth. Alternatively, you can carefully transfer the soup in batches to a blender and blend until smooth.
5. **Add Coconut Milk and Seasonings:**
   - Stir in the coconut milk (or heavy cream) and add the grated ginger (if using), ground cumin, ground nutmeg, salt, and pepper.
   - Simmer for an additional 5 minutes to let the flavors meld.
6. **Serve:**
   - Ladle the soup into bowls and garnish with fresh cilantro or parsley if desired.

Tips:

- For a bit of heat, consider adding a pinch of cayenne pepper.
- You can also garnish with a swirl of coconut milk or a sprinkle of toasted pumpkin seeds.

Enjoy your creamy, comforting Kabocha Squash Soup!

Chestnut Rice (Kuri Gohan)

Ingredients:

- 1 cup short-grain Japanese rice
- 1 cup chestnuts (fresh or peeled, cooked)
- 1 1/4 cups dashi stock (or water)
- 1 tablespoon soy sauce
- 1 tablespoon sake
- 1/2 teaspoon salt
- 1 small piece of kombu (optional, for extra flavor)

Instructions:

1. **Prepare the Chestnuts:**
   - If using fresh chestnuts, cut a small slit in each chestnut and roast them at 375°F (190°C) for 20 minutes. Peel the chestnuts while still warm.
2. **Wash the Rice:**
   - Rinse the rice in cold water until the water runs clear. Drain and let it sit for about 30 minutes.
3. **Cook the Rice:**
   - In a rice cooker or a heavy-bottomed pot, combine the washed rice, dashi stock (or water), soy sauce, sake, and salt.
   - If using kombu, place it in the pot with the rice.
4. **Add Chestnuts:**
   - Gently fold in the chestnuts.
5. **Cook:**
   - If using a rice cooker, start the cooking cycle as usual. If using a pot, bring to a boil, then reduce heat to low, cover, and simmer for 15-20 minutes. Let it sit off the heat for 10 minutes.
6. **Serve:**
   - Fluff the rice with a fork or rice paddle. Serve warm.

Tips:

- You can also add a sprinkle of sesame seeds or chopped scallions for extra flavor.

Enjoy your comforting Chestnut Rice!

Sweet Potato Tempura

Ingredients:

- 1 large sweet potato
- 1 cup all-purpose flour
- 1/2 cup cornstarch
- 1 egg
- 1 cup cold sparkling water (or cold water)
- 1/2 teaspoon baking powder
- Vegetable oil, for frying
- Salt, to taste

Instructions:

1. **Prepare the Sweet Potato:**
    - Peel the sweet potato and slice it into thin rounds or sticks, about 1/4 inch thick. Soak in cold water for 10 minutes, then drain and pat dry.
2. **Make the Tempura Batter:**
    - In a bowl, whisk together the flour, cornstarch, and baking powder.
    - Beat the egg and add it to the dry ingredients.
    - Gradually add the cold sparkling water while stirring gently. The batter should be lumpy.
3. **Heat the Oil:**
    - Heat vegetable oil in a deep skillet or pot to 350°F (175°C).
4. **Coat and Fry:**
    - Dip the sweet potato slices into the tempura batter, allowing excess batter to drip off.
    - Fry in batches, without overcrowding, until golden and crispy, about 2-3 minutes per side.
    - Remove with a slotted spoon and drain on paper towels.
5. **Season and Serve:**
    - Sprinkle with salt while still warm. Serve immediately with dipping sauce, if desired.

Enjoy your crispy Sweet Potato Tempura!

Miso Soup with Mushrooms

Ingredients:

- 4 cups dashi stock (or water)
- 1 cup mushrooms (shiitake, enoki, or any preferred type), sliced
- 1/4 cup miso paste (white or red, depending on preference)
- 2 green onions, chopped
- 1 block of tofu, cubed (optional)
- 1 sheet nori (seaweed), cut into strips (optional)

Instructions:

1. **Prepare the Broth:**
   - Heat the dashi stock in a pot over medium heat until it starts to simmer.
2. **Add the Mushrooms:**
   - Add the sliced mushrooms to the pot and simmer for about 5 minutes, or until tender.
3. **Dissolve the Miso Paste:**
   - In a small bowl, ladle a bit of hot broth and whisk in the miso paste until smooth. Stir this mixture back into the pot.
4. **Add Tofu and Green Onions:**
   - If using tofu, gently add the cubes and heat through for a few minutes. Stir in the chopped green onions.
5. **Finish and Serve:**
   - If desired, add nori strips just before serving for extra flavor and texture. Serve hot.

Enjoy your savory Miso Soup with Mushrooms!

Pumpkin Croquettes

Ingredients:

- 2 cups cooked and mashed pumpkin (or kabocha squash)
- 1 medium onion, finely chopped
- 1/2 cup cooked ground meat (beef or pork) or use a vegetarian substitute
- 1 tablespoon vegetable oil
- 1/4 cup breadcrumbs (plus extra for coating)
- 1/4 cup all-purpose flour
- 1 egg, beaten
- Salt and pepper to taste
- Vegetable oil, for frying

Instructions:

1. **Prepare the Filling:**
   - Heat 1 tablespoon of vegetable oil in a skillet over medium heat.
   - Add the finely chopped onion and cook until translucent.
   - If using ground meat, add it to the skillet and cook until browned. Season with salt and pepper.
   - In a large bowl, combine the cooked onions and meat with the mashed pumpkin. Mix well. Adjust seasoning if necessary.
2. **Shape the Croquettes:**
   - Shape the pumpkin mixture into small patties or balls, about 2 inches in diameter. Flatten slightly if you prefer a patty shape.
3. **Coat the Croquettes:**
   - Set up a breading station: Place flour in one dish, beaten egg in another, and breadcrumbs in a third.
   - Dredge each croquette in flour, dip into the beaten egg, and coat with breadcrumbs, pressing lightly to adhere.
4. **Fry the Croquettes:**
   - Heat vegetable oil in a deep skillet or pot over medium-high heat to about 350°F (175°C).
   - Fry the croquettes in batches until golden brown and crispy, about 3-4 minutes per side.
   - Remove with a slotted spoon and drain on paper towels.
5. **Serve:**
   - Serve the pumpkin croquettes warm with a side of tonkotsu sauce or a dipping sauce of your choice.

Enjoy your crispy and savory Pumpkin Croquettes!

Simmered Daikon Radish

Ingredients:

- 1 large daikon radish (about 1 pound)
- 2 cups dashi stock (or water)
- 2 tablespoons soy sauce
- 2 tablespoons mirin
- 1 tablespoon sugar
- 1 tablespoon sake (optional)
- 1 teaspoon grated ginger (optional)
- 1 scallion, chopped (for garnish, optional)

Instructions:

1. **Prepare the Daikon:**
   - Peel the daikon radish and cut it into thick rounds, about 1/2 inch to 1 inch thick. You can also cut the rounds into quarters if you prefer smaller pieces.
2. **Blanch the Daikon:**
   - Bring a pot of water to a boil. Add the daikon pieces and blanch for about 2-3 minutes. This helps remove any bitterness and makes the daikon absorb the flavors better. Drain and set aside.
3. **Simmer the Daikon:**
   - In a large pot, combine the dashi stock (or water), soy sauce, mirin, sugar, and sake (if using). Bring to a simmer over medium heat.
   - Add the blanched daikon pieces to the pot.
4. **Cook Until Tender:**
   - Cover the pot and let the daikon simmer gently for 20-30 minutes, or until the daikon is tender and has absorbed the flavors. You can use a lid or a piece of parchment paper placed directly on the surface of the daikon to help keep the daikon submerged.
5. **Add Ginger (Optional):**
   - If using, stir in the grated ginger just before serving.
6. **Serve:**
   - Transfer the daikon to serving bowls and spoon some of the cooking liquid over the top. Garnish with chopped scallions if desired.

Enjoy your savory Simmered Daikon Radish!

Japanese Beef Stew

Ingredients:

- 1 lb (450g) beef (chuck or sirloin), cut into bite-sized pieces
- 2 tablespoons vegetable oil
- 1 medium onion, sliced
- 2 medium carrots, sliced
- 2 medium potatoes, peeled and cut into chunks
- 1 cup dashi stock (or water)
- 1/4 cup soy sauce
- 1/4 cup mirin
- 2 tablespoons sugar
- 1 tablespoon sake (optional)
- 2 tablespoons chopped green onions (for garnish, optional)

Instructions:

1. **Prepare the Ingredients:**
   - Cut the beef into bite-sized pieces. Slice the onion, carrots, and potatoes.
2. **Brown the Beef:**
   - Heat vegetable oil in a large pot or Dutch oven over medium heat.
   - Add the beef pieces and brown on all sides, about 5 minutes. Remove the beef from the pot and set aside.
3. **Sauté the Vegetables:**
   - In the same pot, add the sliced onion and cook until softened and translucent, about 5 minutes.
4. **Add the Carrots and Potatoes:**
   - Add the carrots and potatoes to the pot and stir for a few minutes.
5. **Combine Ingredients:**
   - Return the browned beef to the pot. Pour in the dashi stock (or water), soy sauce, mirin, sugar, and sake (if using). Stir to combine.
6. **Simmer:**
   - Bring the mixture to a boil, then reduce heat to low and cover the pot. Simmer for about 30-40 minutes, or until the beef is tender and the vegetables are cooked through.
7. **Adjust Seasoning:**
   - Taste and adjust seasoning if necessary. You can add a bit more soy sauce or sugar depending on your preference.
8. **Serve:**
   - Garnish with chopped green onions if desired. Serve hot over steamed rice or on its own.

Enjoy your delicious Japanese Beef Stew!

Autumn Vegetable Stir-Fry

Ingredients:

- 1 tablespoon vegetable oil
- 1 medium carrot, sliced
- 1 bell pepper, sliced
- 1 cup butternut squash, cubed
- 1 cup broccoli florets
- 1/2 cup mushrooms, sliced
- 2 cloves garlic, minced
- 1 tablespoon ginger, minced
- 3 tablespoons soy sauce
- 1 tablespoon mirin
- 1 tablespoon hoisin sauce (optional)
- 1 teaspoon sesame oil
- 1 tablespoon cornstarch mixed with 2 tablespoons water (for thickening, optional)
- Cooked rice or noodles, for serving

Instructions:

1. **Prepare the Vegetables:**
   - Cut all vegetables into bite-sized pieces.
2. **Heat Oil:**
   - In a large skillet or wok, heat the vegetable oil over medium-high heat.
3. **Cook the Vegetables:**
   - Add the carrots and butternut squash first, stir-fry for about 5 minutes.
   - Add the bell pepper, broccoli, and mushrooms. Stir-fry for another 5 minutes or until all vegetables are tender-crisp.
4. **Add Aromatics:**
   - Push vegetables to one side of the pan. Add garlic and ginger to the empty side, and cook for about 30 seconds until fragrant.
5. **Add Sauce:**
   - Combine soy sauce, mirin, and hoisin sauce (if using). Pour over the vegetables and stir to coat evenly.
6. **Thicken Sauce (Optional):**
   - If you prefer a thicker sauce, stir in the cornstarch mixture and cook for an additional minute until the sauce thickens.
7. **Finish:**
   - Drizzle with sesame oil and mix well.
8. **Serve:**
   - Serve hot over cooked rice or noodles.

Enjoy your flavorful Autumn Vegetable Stir-Fry!

Grilled Salmon with Teriyaki Sauce

Ingredients:

- 4 salmon fillets (about 6 oz each)
- 1/4 cup soy sauce
- 2 tablespoons mirin
- 2 tablespoons sake (or dry white wine)
- 2 tablespoons brown sugar
- 1 garlic clove, minced
- 1 teaspoon fresh ginger, grated
- 1 tablespoon vegetable oil
- Sesame seeds and chopped green onions for garnish (optional)

Instructions:

1. **Prepare the Teriyaki Sauce:**
    - In a small saucepan, combine soy sauce, mirin, sake, brown sugar, garlic, and ginger. Bring to a simmer over medium heat, stirring until the sugar dissolves. Simmer for 5 minutes until slightly thickened. Remove from heat and let cool.
2. **Marinate the Salmon:**
    - Place the salmon fillets in a shallow dish and pour half of the teriyaki sauce over them. Marinate for at least 15 minutes, or up to 1 hour in the refrigerator.
3. **Preheat Grill:**
    - Preheat your grill to medium-high heat. Brush the grill grates with vegetable oil to prevent sticking.
4. **Grill the Salmon:**
    - Remove the salmon from the marinade and discard the used marinade. Grill the salmon for 4-5 minutes per side, or until cooked through and easily flaked with a fork.
5. **Glaze and Serve:**
    - Brush the salmon with some of the reserved teriyaki sauce during the last minute of grilling.
6. **Garnish:**
    - Garnish with sesame seeds and chopped green onions, if desired. Serve with steamed rice or vegetables.

Enjoy your grilled salmon with a delicious teriyaki glaze!

Roasted Sweet Potatoes with Soy Glaze

Ingredients:

- 2 large sweet potatoes, peeled and cut into 1-inch cubes
- 2 tablespoons vegetable oil
- 1/4 cup soy sauce
- 2 tablespoons honey or maple syrup
- 1 tablespoon rice vinegar or apple cider vinegar
- 1 tablespoon sesame oil
- 2 cloves garlic, minced
- 1 teaspoon fresh ginger, grated (optional)
- 1 tablespoon sesame seeds (optional)
- 2 green onions, chopped (optional)

Instructions:

1. **Preheat Oven:**
   - Preheat your oven to 425°F (220°C). Line a baking sheet with parchment paper or lightly grease it.
2. **Prepare the Sweet Potatoes:**
   - In a large bowl, toss the sweet potato cubes with vegetable oil until evenly coated.
3. **Roast the Sweet Potatoes:**
   - Spread the sweet potatoes in a single layer on the prepared baking sheet. Roast for 25-30 minutes, or until tender and golden brown, flipping halfway through.
4. **Prepare the Soy Glaze:**
   - While the sweet potatoes are roasting, in a small saucepan, combine soy sauce, honey (or maple syrup), rice vinegar (or apple cider vinegar), sesame oil, minced garlic, and grated ginger (if using).
   - Bring to a simmer over medium heat, stirring occasionally. Simmer for 3-5 minutes until slightly thickened. Remove from heat and set aside.
5. **Glaze the Sweet Potatoes:**
   - Once the sweet potatoes are roasted, transfer them to a large bowl. Pour the soy glaze over the sweet potatoes and toss to coat evenly.
6. **Garnish and Serve:**
   - Transfer the glazed sweet potatoes to a serving dish. Garnish with sesame seeds and chopped green onions, if desired.

Enjoy your flavorful Roasted Sweet Potatoes with Soy Glaze!

Kinpira Gobo (Braised Burdock Root)

Ingredients:

- 1 large burdock root (about 8 inches), scrubbed and peeled
- 1 medium carrot, peeled
- 2 tablespoons vegetable oil
- 2 tablespoons soy sauce
- 1 tablespoon mirin
- 1 tablespoon sugar
- 1 tablespoon sake (optional)
- 1/4 cup water
- 1 teaspoon sesame seeds (optional)
- 1 teaspoon sesame oil (optional)
- 1-2 green onions, sliced (for garnish, optional)

Instructions:

1. **Prepare the Vegetables:**
   - Cut the burdock root into thin matchstick-sized strips. To prevent discoloration, place the cut burdock root in a bowl of water with a splash of vinegar and let it soak while you prepare the rest of the ingredients.
   - Slice the carrot into thin matchstick-sized strips as well.
2. **Cook the Vegetables:**
   - Heat the vegetable oil in a large skillet or wok over medium heat.
   - Drain the burdock root and add it to the skillet along with the carrot. Stir-fry for 3-4 minutes until the vegetables begin to soften.
3. **Add Seasonings:**
   - Add the soy sauce, mirin, sugar, and sake (if using) to the skillet. Stir to combine and coat the vegetables.
   - Pour in the water, bring to a boil, then reduce the heat to low. Simmer, uncovered, for about 10-15 minutes, or until the liquid has mostly evaporated and the vegetables are tender.
4. **Finish the Dish:**
   - If using, stir in the sesame oil for extra flavor. Garnish with sesame seeds and sliced green onions if desired.
5. **Serve:**
   - Serve warm or at room temperature as a side dish.

Enjoy your savory and slightly sweet Kinpira Gobo!

Soba Noodles with Roasted Pumpkin

Ingredients:

- 1 small pumpkin (or 2 cups cubed butternut squash)
- 2 tablespoons olive oil
- Salt and pepper to taste
- 8 oz soba noodles
- 2 tablespoons soy sauce
- 1 tablespoon mirin
- 1 tablespoon rice vinegar
- 1 tablespoon sesame oil
- 2 cloves garlic, minced
- 2 green onions, sliced
- 1 tablespoon sesame seeds (optional)
- Fresh cilantro or parsley for garnish (optional)

Instructions:

1. **Roast the Pumpkin:**
    - Preheat your oven to 400°F (200°C).
    - Cut the pumpkin into 1-inch cubes and toss with olive oil, salt, and pepper.
    - Spread the cubes on a baking sheet in a single layer and roast for 25-30 minutes, or until tender and caramelized. Stir halfway through.
2. **Cook the Soba Noodles:**
    - While the pumpkin is roasting, bring a large pot of water to a boil.
    - Add the soba noodles and cook according to package instructions, usually 4-6 minutes.
    - Drain the noodles and rinse under cold water to stop the cooking process. Drain well.
3. **Prepare the Sauce:**
    - In a small bowl, mix together soy sauce, mirin, rice vinegar, and sesame oil.
4. **Combine the Noodles and Pumpkin:**
    - In a large bowl, toss the cooked soba noodles with the sauce until evenly coated.
    - Gently fold in the roasted pumpkin.
5. **Finish the Dish:**
    - Stir in the minced garlic (raw or lightly sautéed, depending on your preference) and sliced green onions.
    - Garnish with sesame seeds and fresh herbs if desired.
6. **Serve:**
    - Serve warm or at room temperature.

Enjoy your flavorful Soba Noodles with Roasted Pumpkin!

Japanese Pickled Vegetables

Ingredients:

- 1 cup daikon radish, sliced
- 1 cup cucumber, sliced
- 1 cup carrots, sliced
- 1 cup napa cabbage, chopped (optional)
- 1 tablespoon salt
- 1/2 cup rice vinegar
- 1/2 cup water
- 1/4 cup sugar
- 1 tablespoon soy sauce
- 1 tablespoon mirin
- 1 teaspoon grated ginger (optional)
- 1 teaspoon sesame seeds (optional)
- 1-2 dried red chili peppers (optional, for added heat)

Instructions:

1. **Prepare the Vegetables:**
    - Slice the daikon, cucumber, and carrots into thin rounds or matchstick-sized pieces. Chop the napa cabbage if using.
2. **Salt the Vegetables:**
    - Place the sliced vegetables in a bowl and sprinkle with salt. Toss to coat and let sit for about 30 minutes to draw out excess moisture. This step helps the vegetables become more crisp and flavorful.
3. **Rinse and Drain:**
    - After 30 minutes, rinse the salted vegetables under cold water to remove excess salt. Drain well and pat dry with a clean towel.
4. **Prepare the Pickling Liquid:**
    - In a small saucepan, combine rice vinegar, water, sugar, soy sauce, mirin, and grated ginger (if using). Heat over medium heat, stirring until the sugar is fully dissolved. Remove from heat and let cool.
5. **Pickle the Vegetables:**
    - Place the prepared vegetables into a clean jar or airtight container. Pour the cooled pickling liquid over the vegetables, making sure they are fully submerged. Add dried chili peppers if you like a bit of heat.
6. **Marinate:**
    - Seal the jar or container and refrigerate for at least 24 hours before eating. The pickles will develop more flavor the longer they sit, up to 1 week.
7. **Serve:**
    - Serve the pickled vegetables as a side dish or accompaniment to Japanese meals.

Tips:

- You can vary the vegetables used based on what's in season or your personal preference.
- For a different flavor profile, consider adding a few cloves of garlic or a small piece of kombu (dried seaweed) to the pickling liquid.

Enjoy your homemade Japanese pickled vegetables!

Udon Noodle Soup with Seasonal Veggies

Ingredients:

- 8 oz udon noodles (fresh or dried)
- 4 cups dashi stock (or water, with a dashi packet or miso paste for flavor)
- 2 tablespoons soy sauce
- 2 tablespoons mirin
- 1 tablespoon sake (optional)
- 1 tablespoon vegetable oil
- 1 medium onion, sliced
- 2 cloves garlic, minced
- 1 medium carrot, sliced
- 1 cup mushrooms (shiitake, enoki, or button), sliced
- 1 cup baby spinach or bok choy, chopped
- 1 small zucchini, sliced
- 1 cup seasonal vegetables (e.g., bell peppers, green beans, snap peas), sliced
- 1-2 green onions, chopped
- Sesame seeds for garnish (optional)
- Fresh cilantro or parsley for garnish (optional)
- Soy sauce or additional dashi for seasoning

Instructions:

1. **Prepare the Udon Noodles:**
   - If using dried udon noodles, cook them according to the package instructions. Fresh udon noodles only need to be heated. Drain and set aside.
2. **Prepare the Soup Base:**
   - In a large pot, heat the vegetable oil over medium heat.
   - Add the sliced onion and cook until translucent, about 5 minutes.
   - Add the minced garlic and cook for another 30 seconds until fragrant.
3. **Add Vegetables:**
   - Add the carrot, mushrooms, and any other hardy vegetables (e.g., zucchini). Stir-fry for 3-4 minutes.
4. **Add Stock and Seasonings:**
   - Pour in the dashi stock (or water with a dashi packet or miso paste). Bring to a simmer.
   - Stir in the soy sauce, mirin, and sake (if using). Adjust the seasoning with soy sauce or additional dashi if needed.
5. **Simmer the Soup:**
   - Add the remaining seasonal vegetables (e.g., baby spinach, bok choy) and cook for an additional 2-3 minutes, until vegetables are tender but still crisp.
6. **Add Udon Noodles:**
   - Add the cooked udon noodles to the pot and gently stir to combine. Heat through for 2-3 minutes.

7. **Serve:**
    - Ladle the soup into bowls. Garnish with chopped green onions, sesame seeds, and fresh cilantro or parsley if desired.

Enjoy your comforting and delicious Udon Noodle Soup with Seasonal Vegetables!

Sukiyaki

Ingredients:

- 1 lb (450g) beef (sirloin or ribeye), thinly sliced
- 1 tablespoon vegetable oil
- 1 medium onion, sliced
- 1 cup shiitake mushrooms, sliced
- 1 cup napa cabbage, chopped
- 1 cup tofu, cubed
- 1 cup bamboo shoots (canned or fresh), sliced
- 1 cup shirataki noodles (optional), rinsed
- 4 tablespoons soy sauce
- 4 tablespoons mirin
- 2 tablespoons sugar
- 1/2 cup sake (optional)
- 1 cup dashi stock (or water with a dashi packet)

Instructions:

1. **Prepare the Ingredients:**
   - Slice the beef thinly against the grain. Slice the vegetables and tofu into bite-sized pieces.
2. **Make the Sauce:**
   - In a bowl, combine soy sauce, mirin, sugar, and sake (if using). Stir until the sugar is dissolved. Set aside.
3. **Cook the Beef:**
   - Heat the vegetable oil in a large skillet or Dutch oven over medium heat.
   - Add the sliced onion and cook until softened, about 5 minutes.
   - Add the beef slices and cook until browned, about 2-3 minutes.
4. **Add Vegetables and Tofu:**
   - Add the mushrooms, napa cabbage, tofu, and bamboo shoots to the skillet. Stir to combine.
5. **Add the Sauce and Stock:**
   - Pour the prepared sauce over the beef and vegetables. Add the dashi stock (or water). Bring to a simmer.
6. **Simmer:**
   - Let the sukiyaki simmer gently for about 10-15 minutes, until the vegetables are tender and the flavors meld together. Add the shirataki noodles, if using, during the last 5 minutes of cooking.
7. **Serve:**
   - Serve hot directly from the skillet, allowing diners to pick their favorite ingredients. Enjoy with steamed rice or as part of a larger meal.

Optional:

- For a traditional touch, you can also serve sukiyaki with raw eggs for dipping.

Enjoy your flavorful Sukiyaki!

Japanese Curry Rice with Seasonal Vegetables

Ingredients:

- 1 lb (450g) chicken thighs or beef (cut into bite-sized pieces, optional)
- 2 tablespoons vegetable oil
- 1 large onion, chopped
- 2 cloves garlic, minced
- 1 tablespoon ginger, minced
- 2 medium carrots, peeled and sliced
- 2 medium potatoes, peeled and diced
- 1 cup seasonal vegetables (e.g., bell peppers, zucchini, mushrooms)
- 4 cups water or chicken/vegetable broth
- 1 package (about 7 oz) Japanese curry roux (mild, medium, or hot, depending on preference)
- Cooked rice (for serving)
- Fresh parsley or cilantro (for garnish, optional)

Instructions:

1. **Prepare the Ingredients:**
    - Cut the meat and vegetables into bite-sized pieces.
2. **Cook the Meat:**
    - Heat the vegetable oil in a large pot over medium heat.
    - Add the meat and cook until browned on all sides. Remove the meat from the pot and set aside.
3. **Sauté the Aromatics:**
    - In the same pot, add the chopped onion and cook until softened and translucent, about 5 minutes.
    - Add the minced garlic and ginger and cook for another 30 seconds until fragrant.
4. **Add the Vegetables:**
    - Add the carrots, potatoes, and any other seasonal vegetables you're using. Stir to combine and cook for 5 minutes.
5. **Add the Liquid:**
    - Return the meat to the pot. Pour in the water or broth, bring to a boil, and then reduce heat to a simmer. Cook for about 20 minutes, or until the vegetables are tender and the meat is cooked through.
6. **Add the Curry Roux:**
    - Break the curry roux into pieces and add it to the pot. Stir until the roux is fully dissolved and the sauce thickens, about 5 minutes. If the curry is too thick, you can add a little more water or broth to reach your desired consistency.
7. **Season and Adjust:**
    - Taste the curry and adjust seasoning if needed. You can add a pinch of salt or a bit more curry roux for extra flavor.
8. **Serve:**

- Serve the curry over steamed rice. Garnish with fresh parsley or cilantro if desired.

Enjoy your flavorful Japanese Curry Rice with Seasonal Vegetables!

Tempura Pumpkin and Mushrooms

Ingredients:

- 1 cup pumpkin (or kabocha squash), peeled and sliced into thin wedges
- 1 cup mushrooms (shiitake or button), cleaned and trimmed
- 1 cup all-purpose flour, plus extra for dusting
- 1 large egg
- 1 cup cold sparkling water (or ice-cold water)
- 1/2 teaspoon baking powder
- Vegetable oil, for frying
- Sea salt, for seasoning
- Soy sauce or tempura dipping sauce (for serving)

Instructions:

1. **Prepare the Ingredients:**
   - Slice the pumpkin into thin wedges, about 1/4 inch thick. If using kabocha, you can leave the skin on.
   - Clean and trim the mushrooms.
2. **Make the Tempura Batter:**
   - In a bowl, whisk together the flour, baking powder, and a pinch of salt.
   - In another bowl, beat the egg and then mix in the cold sparkling water.
   - Pour the egg mixture into the flour mixture and gently stir until just combined. The batter should be lumpy; don't overmix.
3. **Heat the Oil:**
   - Heat about 2 inches of vegetable oil in a deep skillet or pot over medium-high heat to 350°F (175°C).
4. **Prepare the Vegetables:**
   - Lightly dust the pumpkin wedges and mushrooms with a bit of flour to help the batter adhere better.
5. **Fry the Tempura:**
   - Dip the vegetables into the tempura batter, allowing excess batter to drip off.
   - Carefully place the battered vegetables into the hot oil. Fry in batches, making sure not to overcrowd the pan.
   - Fry for 2-3 minutes, or until golden brown and crispy. Use a slotted spoon to remove the tempura from the oil and drain on paper towels.
6. **Season and Serve:**
   - Sprinkle with a pinch of sea salt while still hot.
   - Serve with soy sauce or tempura dipping sauce.

Enjoy your crispy Tempura Pumpkin and Mushrooms!

Sweet Potato and Black Sesame Pudding

Ingredients:

- 1 medium sweet potato (about 1 cup mashed)
- 1/2 cup black sesame seeds, toasted and ground
- 1 cup milk (dairy or non-dairy)
- 1/2 cup sugar (adjust to taste)
- 2 tablespoons cornstarch
- 1/2 teaspoon vanilla extract
- Pinch of salt
- Toasted black sesame seeds (for garnish, optional)

Instructions:

1. **Prepare the Sweet Potato:**
    - Peel and chop the sweet potato. Steam or boil until tender, about 15-20 minutes. Drain and mash until smooth. Measure out 1 cup of mashed sweet potato.
2. **Toast and Grind Sesame Seeds:**
    - Toast the black sesame seeds in a dry skillet over medium heat until fragrant, about 2-3 minutes. Let them cool slightly, then grind in a spice grinder or food processor until finely ground.
3. **Prepare the Pudding Base:**
    - In a medium saucepan, combine the ground black sesame seeds, milk, sugar, cornstarch, and a pinch of salt. Whisk until the cornstarch is fully dissolved.
4. **Cook the Pudding:**
    - Place the saucepan over medium heat and cook, stirring constantly, until the mixture starts to thicken and bubble. This should take about 5-7 minutes.
5. **Incorporate Sweet Potato:**
    - Once the pudding has thickened, add the mashed sweet potato and continue to cook, stirring frequently, until the pudding is smooth and thickened to your desired consistency.
6. **Finish the Pudding:**
    - Remove from heat and stir in the vanilla extract. Let the pudding cool slightly.
7. **Serve:**
    - Spoon the pudding into serving dishes or bowls. Chill in the refrigerator for at least 2 hours to set.
8. **Garnish (Optional):**
    - Before serving, garnish with a sprinkle of toasted black sesame seeds for extra flavor and texture.

Enjoy your creamy and flavorful Sweet Potato and Black Sesame Pudding!

Mushroom Rice (Kinoko Gohan)

Ingredients:

- 1 cup short-grain or sushi rice
- 1 1/4 cups water (for cooking rice)
- 1 cup mixed mushrooms (shiitake, enoki, and/or button), sliced
- 1 tablespoon vegetable oil
- 1/2 cup soy sauce
- 1 tablespoon mirin
- 1 tablespoon sake (optional)
- 1 teaspoon sugar
- 2 green onions, chopped (for garnish, optional)
- Fresh parsley or cilantro, chopped (for garnish, optional)

Instructions:

1. **Rinse the Rice:**
   - Rinse the rice under cold water until the water runs clear. Drain well.
2. **Prepare the Mushrooms:**
   - Heat the vegetable oil in a skillet over medium heat.
   - Add the sliced mushrooms and sauté until tender and browned, about 5-7 minutes.
3. **Season the Mushrooms:**
   - Add the soy sauce, mirin, sake (if using), and sugar to the mushrooms. Cook for another 2-3 minutes until the sauce is absorbed and mushrooms are well-seasoned. Set aside.
4. **Cook the Rice:**
   - In a rice cooker or a medium saucepan, add the rinsed rice and 1 1/4 cups water. Cook according to your rice cooker's instructions or bring to a boil, then reduce heat to low, cover, and simmer for 18-20 minutes until the rice is tender and water is absorbed.
5. **Combine:**
   - Once the rice is cooked, gently fold in the sautéed mushrooms with their sauce. Mix until evenly distributed.
6. **Garnish and Serve:**
   - Garnish with chopped green onions and fresh parsley or cilantro if desired. Serve warm.

Enjoy your flavorful Mushroom Rice (Kinoko Gohan)!

Teriyaki Chicken with Grilled Autumn Vegetables

Ingredients:

For the Teriyaki Chicken:

- 4 boneless, skinless chicken thighs or breasts
- 1/4 cup soy sauce
- 2 tablespoons mirin
- 2 tablespoons sake (optional)
- 2 tablespoons honey or brown sugar
- 1 clove garlic, minced
- 1 teaspoon fresh ginger, grated
- 1 tablespoon vegetable oil

For the Grilled Autumn Vegetables:

- 1 small butternut squash, peeled and cubed
- 1 red bell pepper, sliced
- 1 cup Brussels sprouts, halved
- 1 tablespoon olive oil
- Salt and pepper to taste
- 1 teaspoon dried rosemary or thyme (optional)

Instructions:

1. **Marinate the Chicken:**
   - In a bowl, mix soy sauce, mirin, sake (if using), honey, garlic, and ginger.
   - Add the chicken to the marinade and let it sit for at least 30 minutes, or up to 2 hours in the refrigerator.
2. **Prepare the Vegetables:**
   - Preheat your grill to medium-high heat.
   - Toss the butternut squash, bell pepper, and Brussels sprouts with olive oil, salt, pepper, and dried rosemary or thyme (if using).
3. **Grill the Vegetables:**
   - Place the vegetables on the grill and cook, turning occasionally, until tender and slightly charred, about 15-20 minutes. Remove and keep warm.
4. **Cook the Chicken:**
   - Heat vegetable oil in a grill pan or on the grill over medium heat.
   - Remove the chicken from the marinade and grill for about 5-7 minutes per side, or until fully cooked and an internal temperature of 165°F (74°C) is reached. Baste with the marinade occasionally while cooking.
5. **Serve:**
   - Slice the grilled chicken and serve with the grilled autumn vegetables.

Enjoy your Teriyaki Chicken with Grilled Autumn Vegetables!

Roasted Chestnut Soup

Ingredients:

- 1 lb (450g) fresh chestnuts
- 2 tablespoons olive oil
- 1 large onion, chopped
- 2 cloves garlic, minced
- 2 medium carrots, peeled and diced
- 2 celery stalks, diced
- 4 cups vegetable or chicken broth
- 1 cup milk or cream (or a non-dairy alternative)
- 1 teaspoon fresh thyme leaves (or 1/2 teaspoon dried thyme)
- 1 bay leaf
- Salt and pepper to taste
- 2 tablespoons butter or additional olive oil
- Chopped fresh parsley or chives for garnish (optional)

Instructions:

1. **Prepare the Chestnuts:**
   - Preheat your oven to 425°F (220°C).
   - With a sharp knife, cut an "X" on the flat side of each chestnut.
   - Place the chestnuts on a baking sheet and roast for 15-20 minutes, or until the skins start to peel back and the nuts are tender.
   - Remove from the oven and let cool slightly. Peel the chestnuts while they are still warm, removing both the outer shell and the thin brown skin.
2. **Make the Soup Base:**
   - Heat olive oil in a large pot over medium heat.
   - Add the chopped onion and cook until translucent, about 5 minutes.
   - Add the minced garlic and cook for an additional 1 minute until fragrant.
   - Stir in the diced carrots and celery, cooking until the vegetables start to soften, about 5-7 minutes.
3. **Add the Chestnuts and Broth:**
   - Add the peeled chestnuts to the pot. Stir to combine.
   - Pour in the broth, add the thyme and bay leaf, and bring to a simmer.
   - Simmer for 20-25 minutes, until the vegetables and chestnuts are tender.
4. **Blend the Soup:**
   - Remove the bay leaf. Use an immersion blender to puree the soup until smooth. Alternatively, carefully transfer the soup in batches to a blender, blend until smooth, and return to the pot.
5. **Finish the Soup:**
   - Stir in the milk or cream. Heat through, but do not boil. Adjust seasoning with salt and pepper to taste.
   - If using, stir in butter for added richness.

6. **Serve:**
    - Ladle the soup into bowls and garnish with chopped fresh parsley or chives if desired.

Enjoy your rich and comforting Roasted Chestnut Soup!

Sweet Potato and Caramelized Onion Pizza

Ingredients:

For the Pizza Dough:

- 2 1/4 teaspoons active dry yeast (1 packet)
- 1 1/2 cups warm water (110°F/45°C)
- 3 1/2 cups all-purpose flour
- 2 tablespoons olive oil
- 1 teaspoon salt
- 1 teaspoon sugar

For the Topping:

- 1 large sweet potato, peeled and thinly sliced
- 2 tablespoons olive oil
- 2 large onions, thinly sliced
- 1 tablespoon brown sugar
- 1 teaspoon balsamic vinegar
- 1 1/2 cups shredded mozzarella cheese
- 1/2 cup crumbled feta cheese
- Fresh thyme leaves or rosemary (for garnish)
- Salt and pepper to taste

Instructions:

1. **Prepare the Dough:**
    - In a small bowl, dissolve yeast and sugar in warm water. Let sit for about 5-10 minutes until frothy.
    - In a large bowl, mix flour and salt. Create a well in the center and add the yeast mixture and olive oil. Mix until a dough forms.
    - Knead the dough on a floured surface for about 5-7 minutes until smooth and elastic. Place in a lightly oiled bowl, cover with a damp cloth, and let rise in a warm place for about 1 hour, or until doubled in size.
2. **Caramelize the Onions:**
    - Heat olive oil in a skillet over medium heat. Add the sliced onions and cook, stirring occasionally, for about 15-20 minutes until they are soft and golden brown.
    - Stir in the brown sugar and balsamic vinegar, cooking for another 5 minutes until the onions are caramelized. Remove from heat and set aside.
3. **Prepare the Sweet Potato:**
    - Preheat your oven to 425°F (220°C).
    - Toss the sweet potato slices with olive oil, salt, and pepper. Arrange in a single layer on a baking sheet.

- Roast for about 15-20 minutes until tender, turning halfway through. Set aside.
4. **Assemble the Pizza:**
    - Preheat your oven with a pizza stone or baking sheet inside at 475°F (245°C).
    - Punch down the dough and divide into two portions. Roll out each portion on a floured surface to your desired thickness.
    - Transfer the rolled dough to a pizza peel or parchment paper.
    - Spread a thin layer of mozzarella cheese over the dough. Top with roasted sweet potato slices and caramelized onions.
    - Sprinkle with crumbled feta cheese.
5. **Bake the Pizza:**
    - Transfer the pizza to the preheated pizza stone or baking sheet.
    - Bake for 12-15 minutes until the crust is golden and the cheese is melted and bubbly.
6. **Garnish and Serve:**
    - Remove from the oven and garnish with fresh thyme leaves or rosemary.
    - Slice and serve warm.

Enjoy your Sweet Potato and Caramelized Onion Pizza!

Steamed Egg Custard (Chawanmushi)

Ingredients:

- 4 large eggs
- 1 1/2 cups dashi stock (or substitute with chicken or vegetable broth)
- 1 tablespoon soy sauce
- 1 tablespoon mirin
- 1/2 teaspoon salt
- 1/2 cup cooked chicken (shredded or diced, optional)
- 1/4 cup cooked shrimp (chopped, optional)
- 1/4 cup sliced mushrooms (shiitake or button, optional)
- 1/4 cup blanched green peas or thinly sliced vegetables (optional)
- Fresh cilantro or chives for garnish (optional)

Instructions:

1. **Prepare the Custard Base:**
   - In a bowl, whisk together the eggs until well beaten.
   - Add the dashi stock, soy sauce, mirin, and salt to the eggs, and mix well.
2. **Prepare the Ingredients:**
   - If using, divide the chicken, shrimp, mushrooms, and vegetables among small heatproof cups or ramekins.
3. **Strain the Mixture:**
   - Strain the egg mixture through a fine mesh sieve into a measuring cup or bowl to ensure a smooth texture.
4. **Assemble the Chawanmushi:**
   - Pour the strained egg mixture evenly into the prepared cups or ramekins over the ingredients.
5. **Steam the Custard:**
   - Place the cups in a steamer or a large pot fitted with a steaming rack.
   - Cover with a lid or foil to prevent water from dripping into the custard.
   - Steam over simmering water for about 15-20 minutes, or until the custard is set and a toothpick inserted in the center comes out clean.
6. **Serve:**
   - Carefully remove the cups from the steamer.
   - Garnish with fresh cilantro or chives if desired.

Enjoy your silky and savory Chawanmushi!

Miso Glazed Eggplant

Ingredients:

- 2 medium eggplants
- 2 tablespoons miso paste (white or red)
- 2 tablespoons soy sauce
- 2 tablespoons mirin
- 1 tablespoon sugar
- 1 tablespoon rice vinegar
- 2 teaspoons sesame oil
- 1 tablespoon vegetable oil
- Sesame seeds and chopped green onions for garnish (optional)

Instructions:

1. **Prepare the Eggplant:**
    - Preheat your oven to 400°F (200°C).
    - Cut the eggplants in half lengthwise. Score the flesh in a crosshatch pattern to help the glaze penetrate.
    - Brush the cut sides of the eggplant with vegetable oil.
2. **Roast the Eggplant:**
    - Place the eggplants cut-side up on a baking sheet.
    - Roast for 20-25 minutes until the flesh is tender and lightly browned.
3. **Prepare the Miso Glaze:**
    - In a small bowl, whisk together the miso paste, soy sauce, mirin, sugar, rice vinegar, and sesame oil until smooth.
4. **Glaze the Eggplant:**
    - Remove the eggplants from the oven and brush the miso glaze evenly over the cut sides.
    - Return to the oven and roast for an additional 10 minutes, or until the glaze is bubbly and slightly caramelized.
5. **Garnish and Serve:**
    - Sprinkle with sesame seeds and chopped green onions if desired.
    - Serve warm as a side dish or main course.

Enjoy your flavorful Miso Glazed Eggplant!

Japanese Style Beef and Potato Stew

Ingredients:

- 1 lb (450g) beef (sliced thinly, such as sirloin or chuck)
- 2 tablespoons vegetable oil
- 1 large onion, sliced
- 2 medium potatoes, peeled and cut into bite-sized pieces
- 2 medium carrots, peeled and sliced
- 1 cup shirataki noodles (optional), rinsed
- 2 cups dashi stock (or beef or vegetable broth)
- 1/4 cup soy sauce
- 1/4 cup mirin
- 2 tablespoons sugar
- 1 tablespoon sake (optional)
- 2 green onions, chopped (for garnish, optional)
- Fresh parsley or cilantro (for garnish, optional)

Instructions:

1. **Prepare the Ingredients:**
    - Slice the beef into thin strips.
    - Peel and cut the potatoes and carrots. If using shirataki noodles, rinse them under cold water.
2. **Sauté the Beef and Onions:**
    - Heat vegetable oil in a large pot over medium heat.
    - Add the sliced onion and cook until softened, about 5 minutes.
    - Add the beef and cook until browned on all sides.
3. **Add Vegetables:**
    - Stir in the potatoes and carrots, cooking for another 5 minutes.
4. **Add Stock and Seasonings:**
    - Pour in the dashi stock (or broth), soy sauce, mirin, sugar, and sake (if using). Stir to combine.
    - Bring to a boil, then reduce heat to low and cover.
5. **Simmer:**
    - Simmer for about 20-25 minutes, or until the potatoes and carrots are tender.
    - If using shirataki noodles, add them during the last 5 minutes of cooking.
6. **Adjust Seasoning:**
    - Taste and adjust seasoning if needed. You can add more soy sauce or a bit of sugar according to your taste.
7. **Serve:**
    - Garnish with chopped green onions or fresh parsley/cilantro if desired.
    - Serve hot with steamed rice.

Enjoy your flavorful and comforting Japanese Style Beef and Potato Stew (Nikujaga)!

Apple and Daikon Salad

Ingredients:

- 1 medium daikon radish, peeled and julienned
- 1 large apple, cored and julienned (use a crisp variety like Fuji or Granny Smith)
- 1/4 cup fresh cilantro or parsley, chopped
- 2 tablespoons rice vinegar
- 1 tablespoon soy sauce
- 1 tablespoon honey or sugar
- 1 tablespoon sesame oil
- 1 teaspoon grated ginger (optional)
- 1 tablespoon sesame seeds (for garnish)
- Salt and pepper to taste

Instructions:

1. **Prepare the Vegetables and Fruit:**
   - Peel and julienne the daikon radish.
   - Core and julienne the apple, leaving the skin on for added color and texture.
2. **Make the Dressing:**
   - In a small bowl, whisk together the rice vinegar, soy sauce, honey (or sugar), sesame oil, and grated ginger (if using).
3. **Combine Ingredients:**
   - In a large bowl, toss the julienned daikon radish and apple with the chopped cilantro or parsley.
   - Pour the dressing over the salad and toss gently to combine.
4. **Garnish and Serve:**
   - Sprinkle sesame seeds over the top.
   - Season with salt and pepper to taste.

Serve the salad immediately for the freshest flavor, or chill briefly before serving. Enjoy this crisp and tangy Apple and Daikon Salad!

Spicy Miso Ramen with Seasonal Vegetables

Ingredients:

For the Broth:

- 4 cups chicken or vegetable broth
- 1/4 cup miso paste (red or white)
- 2 tablespoons soy sauce
- 1 tablespoon sesame oil
- 1 tablespoon chili paste or sauce (adjust to taste)
- 2 cloves garlic, minced
- 1 teaspoon fresh ginger, minced
- 1 tablespoon rice vinegar

For the Ramen:

- 2 packs of ramen noodles (fresh or dried)
- 1 cup sliced mushrooms (shiitake, button, or your choice)
- 1 medium carrot, julienned
- 1 cup baby spinach or bok choy
- 1/2 cup corn kernels (fresh or frozen)
- 1/2 cup snow peas or snap peas
- 2 green onions, sliced
- 2 tablespoons vegetable oil

For Toppings:

- 2 soft-boiled eggs (cooked to your preference)
- 1 tablespoon sesame seeds
- Fresh cilantro or parsley (for garnish)
- Nori sheets or seaweed (optional)

Instructions:

1. **Prepare the Broth:**
   - In a large pot, heat sesame oil over medium heat.
   - Add the minced garlic and ginger, cooking for 1-2 minutes until fragrant.
   - Stir in the miso paste, soy sauce, and chili paste, cooking for another minute.
   - Pour in the chicken or vegetable broth and bring to a simmer.
   - Add rice vinegar and adjust seasoning to taste. Simmer for 10-15 minutes to allow the flavors to meld.
2. **Prepare the Vegetables:**
   - In a skillet, heat vegetable oil over medium heat.
   - Add the sliced mushrooms and cook until softened, about 5 minutes.
   - Add the julienned carrot and cook for another 2-3 minutes.

- Stir in the snow peas and corn, cooking for an additional 2 minutes.
- Add the baby spinach or bok choy and cook until wilted. Set aside.
3. **Cook the Ramen Noodles:**
    - Cook the ramen noodles according to package instructions. Drain and set aside.
4. **Assemble the Ramen:**
    - Divide the cooked noodles between bowls.
    - Ladle the hot miso broth over the noodles.
    - Top with the sautéed vegetables.
5. **Add Toppings:**
    - Slice the soft-boiled eggs in half and place on top of the ramen.
    - Sprinkle with sesame seeds and sliced green onions.
    - Garnish with fresh cilantro or parsley and nori sheets if desired.

Enjoy your flavorful and spicy Miso Ramen with Seasonal Vegetables!

Roasted Kabocha and Garlic

Ingredients:

- 1 small kabocha squash, peeled, seeded, and cut into wedges
- 6 cloves garlic, peeled and left whole
- 2 tablespoons olive oil
- 1 teaspoon dried thyme or rosemary (optional)
- Salt and pepper to taste
- Fresh parsley or cilantro for garnish (optional)

Instructions:

1. **Preheat the Oven:**
   - Preheat your oven to 425°F (220°C).
2. **Prepare the Kabocha:**
   - Peel the kabocha squash and remove the seeds. Cut into wedges or bite-sized pieces.
3. **Season:**
   - In a large bowl, toss the kabocha wedges and whole garlic cloves with olive oil, salt, pepper, and dried thyme or rosemary if using.
4. **Roast:**
   - Spread the seasoned kabocha and garlic in a single layer on a baking sheet.
   - Roast for 25-30 minutes, or until the kabocha is tender and caramelized, turning once halfway through.
5. **Serve:**
   - Garnish with chopped fresh parsley or cilantro if desired.

Enjoy your Roasted Kabocha and Garlic as a tasty side dish or snack!

Warm Tofu Salad with Autumn Vegetables

Ingredients:

For the Salad:

- 1 block (14 oz) firm tofu, drained and pressed
- 2 tablespoons vegetable oil (for frying)
- 1 medium sweet potato, peeled and cubed
- 1 cup Brussels sprouts, halved
- 1 medium carrot, peeled and sliced
- 2 cups baby spinach or mixed greens
- 1 red bell pepper, sliced
- 1/4 cup sliced almonds or toasted sesame seeds (optional, for garnish)
- Fresh cilantro or parsley for garnish (optional)

For the Dressing:

- 3 tablespoons soy sauce
- 2 tablespoons rice vinegar
- 1 tablespoon honey or maple syrup
- 1 tablespoon sesame oil
- 1 teaspoon grated fresh ginger
- 1 clove garlic, minced
- 1 teaspoon toasted sesame seeds (optional)

Instructions:

1. **Prepare the Tofu:**
     - Cut the pressed tofu into cubes.
     - Heat vegetable oil in a large skillet over medium heat.
     - Add the tofu cubes and cook, turning occasionally, until golden and crispy on all sides, about 8-10 minutes. Remove from the skillet and set aside.
2. **Roast the Vegetables:**
     - Preheat your oven to 425°F (220°C).
     - On a baking sheet, toss the sweet potato cubes, Brussels sprouts, and carrot slices with a bit of oil, salt, and pepper.
     - Roast for 20-25 minutes, or until the vegetables are tender and caramelized, stirring halfway through.
3. **Prepare the Dressing:**
     - In a small bowl, whisk together soy sauce, rice vinegar, honey (or maple syrup), sesame oil, grated ginger, minced garlic, and toasted sesame seeds (if using).
4. **Assemble the Salad:**
     - In a large bowl, combine the roasted vegetables and crispy tofu.
     - Add the baby spinach or mixed greens and gently toss to combine.

5. **Add the Dressing:**
    - Pour the dressing over the salad and toss until everything is well coated.
6. **Garnish and Serve:**
    - Garnish with sliced almonds or toasted sesame seeds, and fresh cilantro or parsley if desired.
    - Serve warm.

Enjoy your warm and hearty Tofu Salad with Autumn Vegetables!

Nabe Hot Pot with Fall Ingredients

Ingredients:

For the Broth:

- 4 cups dashi stock (or substitute with chicken or vegetable broth)
- 1/4 cup soy sauce
- 2 tablespoons mirin
- 1 tablespoon sake (optional)
- 1 tablespoon miso paste (optional for extra flavor)

For the Hot Pot:

- 1/2 lb (225g) thinly sliced beef, pork, or chicken
- 1 small kabocha squash, peeled and cut into bite-sized pieces
- 1 cup shiitake or other mushrooms, sliced
- 1 cup daikon radish, peeled and sliced
- 1 cup carrots, peeled and sliced
- 1 cup baby bok choy or spinach
- 1 cup tofu, cut into cubes
- 1 cup cooked soba or udon noodles (optional)
- 2 green onions, sliced (for garnish)
- Fresh cilantro or parsley (for garnish)

Instructions:

1. **Prepare the Broth:**
    - In a large pot or hot pot, combine the dashi stock, soy sauce, mirin, and sake. If using miso paste, stir it in until dissolved. Heat the broth until it begins to simmer.
2. **Prepare the Ingredients:**
    - Slice the vegetables and proteins into bite-sized pieces. Arrange them on a platter for easy access.
3. **Cook the Hot Pot:**
    - Bring the broth to a gentle simmer at the table or on the stove.
    - Add the tougher vegetables first, such as kabocha squash, daikon radish, and carrots. Cook for 5-7 minutes until they start to soften.
    - Add mushrooms and tofu, cooking for another 5 minutes.
    - Add the sliced meat and cook until just cooked through, about 2-3 minutes.
    - If using noodles, add them last to heat through, about 1-2 minutes.
4. **Serve:**
    - Ladle the hot pot ingredients into bowls, ensuring a good mix of vegetables, protein, and broth.
    - Garnish with sliced green onions and fresh cilantro or parsley.

Enjoy your warm and hearty Nabe Hot Pot with Fall Ingredients!

Japanese Style Sweet Potato Pie

Ingredients:

For the Crust:

- 1 1/2 cups graham cracker crumbs
- 1/4 cup granulated sugar
- 1/4 cup melted butter

For the Filling:

- 2 medium sweet potatoes (about 2 cups mashed)
- 1/2 cup granulated sugar
- 1/4 cup brown sugar
- 1/4 cup heavy cream
- 1/4 cup milk
- 2 large eggs
- 1 teaspoon vanilla extract
- 1/2 teaspoon ground cinnamon
- 1/4 teaspoon ground nutmeg
- Pinch of salt

For the Topping (optional):

- Whipped cream or sweetened whipped cream

Instructions:

1. **Prepare the Crust:**
    - Preheat your oven to 350°F (175°C).
    - In a bowl, mix graham cracker crumbs, sugar, and melted butter until well combined.
    - Press the mixture into the bottom and up the sides of a 9-inch pie dish.
    - Bake the crust for 10 minutes, then let it cool.
2. **Prepare the Sweet Potatoes:**
    - Peel and cut the sweet potatoes into chunks. Boil in a pot of water until tender, about 15-20 minutes.
    - Drain and mash until smooth. You should have about 2 cups of mashed sweet potatoes.
3. **Prepare the Filling:**
    - In a large bowl, whisk together granulated sugar, brown sugar, cream, milk, eggs, vanilla extract, cinnamon, nutmeg, and salt until smooth.
    - Fold in the mashed sweet potatoes until well combined.
4. **Assemble and Bake:**
    - Pour the sweet potato filling into the cooled pie crust.

        - Bake for 45-50 minutes, or until the filling is set and a knife inserted into the center comes out clean.
        - Let the pie cool completely before serving.
5. **Serve:**
        - Top with whipped cream if desired.

Enjoy your Japanese Style Sweet Potato Pie, a sweet and creamy dessert with a unique twist!

Roasted Acorn Squash with Miso Butter

Ingredients:

For the Acorn Squash:

- 2 acorn squash
- 2 tablespoons olive oil
- 1/2 teaspoon salt
- 1/4 teaspoon black pepper

For the Miso Butter:

- 1/4 cup unsalted butter, softened
- 2 tablespoons white or red miso paste
- 1 tablespoon honey or maple syrup
- 1 teaspoon soy sauce
- 1/2 teaspoon grated fresh ginger (optional)
- 1 teaspoon sesame seeds (optional, for garnish)
- Chopped green onions or fresh parsley (optional, for garnish)

Instructions:

1. **Prepare the Acorn Squash:**
   - Preheat your oven to 400°F (200°C).
   - Cut the acorn squash in half lengthwise and scoop out the seeds.
   - Cut each half into wedges or leave in halves for a more rustic presentation.
   - Brush the cut sides with olive oil and season with salt and pepper.
2. **Roast the Squash:**
   - Place the squash halves or wedges cut-side down on a baking sheet lined with parchment paper.
   - Roast for 25-30 minutes, or until the squash is tender and caramelized. The edges should be golden brown and slightly crispy.
3. **Prepare the Miso Butter:**
   - In a small bowl, mix together the softened butter, miso paste, honey or maple syrup, soy sauce, and grated ginger (if using) until smooth and well combined.
4. **Finish and Serve:**
   - Once the squash is done roasting, remove from the oven and flip the pieces cut-side up.
   - Spread a generous amount of miso butter over each piece of squash while still warm. The butter will melt and infuse the squash with flavor.
   - Garnish with sesame seeds and chopped green onions or parsley if desired.

Serve warm and enjoy the rich, savory-sweet flavor of Roasted Acorn Squash with Miso Butter!

Japanese Pumpkin and Coconut Curry

Ingredients:

For the Curry:

- 1 medium kabocha squash or Japanese pumpkin (about 2 cups), peeled, seeded, and cut into cubes
- 1 tablespoon vegetable oil
- 1 medium onion, chopped
- 2 cloves garlic, minced
- 1 tablespoon fresh ginger, minced
- 2 tablespoons curry powder (Japanese curry powder or mild curry powder)
- 1 tablespoon soy sauce
- 1 tablespoon miso paste (white or red)
- 1 can (14 oz) coconut milk
- 1 cup vegetable broth (or chicken broth)
- 1 large carrot, peeled and sliced
- 1 cup bell pepper, sliced (red, green, or yellow)
- 1 tablespoon brown sugar (optional, adjust to taste)
- Salt and pepper to taste
- Cooked rice, for serving

Instructions:

1. **Prepare the Pumpkin:**
   - Peel and cut the kabocha squash or Japanese pumpkin into bite-sized cubes. Set aside.
2. **Cook the Base:**
   - Heat vegetable oil in a large pot or Dutch oven over medium heat.
   - Add the chopped onion and cook until softened and translucent, about 5 minutes.
   - Stir in the minced garlic and ginger, cooking for another minute until fragrant.
3. **Add Spices and Vegetables:**
   - Stir in the curry powder, soy sauce, and miso paste, cooking for 1-2 minutes to toast the spices.
   - Add the kabocha squash cubes, carrot slices, and bell pepper to the pot.
4. **Add Liquids:**
   - Pour in the coconut milk and vegetable broth, stirring to combine.
   - Bring to a gentle simmer and cook for 15-20 minutes, or until the squash and carrots are tender.
5. **Season and Adjust:**
   - Taste and adjust seasoning with salt, pepper, and brown sugar if needed. The curry should have a balanced sweetness and richness.
6. **Serve:**
   - Serve the curry hot over cooked rice.

Enjoy your comforting and flavorful Japanese Pumpkin and Coconut Curry!

Fried Chicken with Apple Slaw

Ingredients:

For the Fried Chicken:

- 4 bone-in, skin-on chicken thighs
- 1 cup buttermilk
- 1 cup all-purpose flour
- 1 teaspoon paprika
- 1 teaspoon garlic powder
- 1 teaspoon onion powder
- 1/2 teaspoon cayenne pepper (optional, for extra heat)
- Salt and pepper to taste
- Vegetable oil, for frying

For the Apple Slaw:

- 1 large apple, cored and thinly sliced (use a crisp variety like Fuji or Granny Smith)
- 2 cups shredded cabbage (green, red, or a mix)
- 1 large carrot, peeled and grated
- 1/4 cup mayonnaise
- 2 tablespoons apple cider vinegar
- 1 tablespoon honey
- 1 teaspoon Dijon mustard
- Salt and pepper to taste
- 1 tablespoon chopped fresh parsley (optional, for garnish)

Instructions:

1. **Marinate the Chicken:**
    - Place the chicken thighs in a bowl and cover with buttermilk. Marinate in the refrigerator for at least 1 hour or overnight for best results.
2. **Prepare the Flour Coating:**
    - In a shallow dish, mix together the flour, paprika, garlic powder, onion powder, cayenne pepper (if using), salt, and pepper.
3. **Coat the Chicken:**
    - Remove the chicken from the buttermilk, allowing excess to drip off.
    - Dredge each piece of chicken in the seasoned flour mixture, pressing lightly to adhere.
4. **Fry the Chicken:**
    - Heat vegetable oil in a large skillet or Dutch oven over medium-high heat to 350°F (175°C). There should be enough oil to cover about halfway up the chicken.

- Fry the chicken in batches, being careful not to overcrowd the pan, until golden brown and cooked through, about 8-10 minutes per side. Use a meat thermometer to ensure the internal temperature reaches 165°F (74°C).
- Drain the fried chicken on a paper towel-lined plate.

5. **Prepare the Apple Slaw:**
    - In a large bowl, combine the sliced apple, shredded cabbage, and grated carrot.
    - In a small bowl, whisk together the mayonnaise, apple cider vinegar, honey, Dijon mustard, salt, and pepper.
    - Pour the dressing over the slaw and toss to coat evenly.
    - Garnish with chopped parsley if desired.
6. **Serve:**
    - Serve the fried chicken hot with a generous helping of apple slaw on the side.

Enjoy your crispy Fried Chicken with a refreshing Apple Slaw!

Grilled Mackerel with Fall Vegetables

Ingredients:

For the Mackerel:

- 4 mackerel fillets (about 6 ounces each)
- 2 tablespoons olive oil
- 2 cloves garlic, minced
- 1 tablespoon fresh lemon juice
- 1 teaspoon dried thyme (or 1 tablespoon fresh thyme leaves)
- Salt and pepper to taste

For the Fall Vegetables:

- 2 cups butternut squash, peeled and cubed
- 1 cup Brussels sprouts, trimmed and halved
- 1 red bell pepper, sliced
- 1 medium red onion, sliced
- 2 tablespoons olive oil
- 1 teaspoon dried rosemary (or 1 tablespoon fresh rosemary leaves)
- Salt and pepper to taste

Instructions:

1. **Prepare the Vegetables:**
    - Preheat your oven to 425°F (220°C).
    - In a large bowl, toss the butternut squash, Brussels sprouts, red bell pepper, and red onion with olive oil, rosemary, salt, and pepper.
    - Spread the vegetables in a single layer on a baking sheet.
    - Roast in the oven for about 25-30 minutes, or until the vegetables are tender and caramelized, stirring halfway through for even cooking.
2. **Prepare the Mackerel:**
    - While the vegetables are roasting, prepare the mackerel. Preheat your grill to medium-high heat.
    - In a small bowl, mix the olive oil, minced garlic, lemon juice, thyme, salt, and pepper.
    - Brush the mackerel fillets with the olive oil mixture on both sides.
    - Place the fillets on the grill and cook for 3-4 minutes per side, or until the fish is opaque and flakes easily with a fork.
3. **Serve:**
    - Once the vegetables are done, remove them from the oven and transfer to a serving platter.
    - Place the grilled mackerel fillets on the platter with the vegetables.

- Optionally, you can garnish with additional fresh thyme or rosemary and a squeeze of lemon juice.

Tips:

- You can use other fall vegetables like sweet potatoes or carrots if you prefer.
- For extra flavor, try adding a splash of balsamic vinegar to the roasted vegetables before serving.

Enjoy your flavorful and hearty grilled mackerel with fall vegetables!

Pickled Sweet Potatoes

Ingredients:

- 2 large sweet potatoes
- 1 cup apple cider vinegar
- 1 cup water
- 1/2 cup granulated sugar
- 2 tablespoons salt
- 2 cloves garlic, sliced
- 1 tablespoon mustard seeds
- 1 teaspoon black peppercorns
- 1/2 teaspoon red pepper flakes (optional, for a bit of heat)
- 1 bay leaf
- 1 small onion, thinly sliced (optional)
- Fresh herbs like dill or thyme (optional)

Instructions:

1. **Prepare the Sweet Potatoes:**
   - Peel the sweet potatoes and cut them into bite-sized cubes or slices, depending on your preference.
   - Bring a large pot of water to a boil and blanch the sweet potatoes for about 3-4 minutes, until just tender but still firm. This step helps maintain their texture after pickling.
   - Drain and let the sweet potatoes cool completely.
2. **Prepare the Brine:**
   - In a medium saucepan, combine the apple cider vinegar, water, sugar, and salt.
   - Bring the mixture to a boil, stirring occasionally until the sugar and salt are dissolved.
   - Add the sliced garlic, mustard seeds, black peppercorns, red pepper flakes (if using), and bay leaf to the brine. Let it simmer for an additional 2-3 minutes.
3. **Pack the Jars:**
   - Sterilize your canning jars and lids by boiling them in water for a few minutes or running them through the dishwasher.
   - Pack the cooled sweet potatoes into the sterilized jars, layering with optional onions and fresh herbs if using.
4. **Add the Brine:**
   - Pour the hot brine over the sweet potatoes in the jars, making sure the vegetables are completely submerged.
   - Wipe the rims of the jars with a clean cloth to remove any residue.
   - Seal the jars with the lids.
5. **Cool and Store:**
   - Allow the jars to cool to room temperature.

- Once cooled, refrigerate the jars. The pickled sweet potatoes will be ready to eat in about 24 hours but will develop more flavor if allowed to sit for a few days.

Tips:

- These pickled sweet potatoes should be kept in the refrigerator and are best consumed within 2-3 weeks.
- For a more intense flavor, you can experiment with additional spices like coriander seeds or cinnamon sticks.

Enjoy your pickled sweet potatoes as a tangy snack, a unique side dish, or as a crunchy addition to salads and sandwiches!

Kabocha and Mushroom Risotto

Ingredients:

- 1 small kabocha squash (about 1-1.5 lbs), peeled, seeded, and cubed
- 2 tablespoons olive oil
- 1 medium onion, finely chopped
- 2 cloves garlic, minced
- 8 ounces mushrooms (e.g., cremini, shiitake, or button), sliced
- 1 1/2 cups Arborio rice
- 1/2 cup dry white wine
- 4 cups vegetable or chicken broth, kept warm
- 1/2 cup grated Parmesan cheese
- 2 tablespoons unsalted butter
- Salt and pepper to taste
- Fresh thyme or parsley, for garnish (optional)

Instructions:

1. **Prepare the Kabocha:**
    - Preheat your oven to 400°F (200°C).
    - Toss the kabocha squash cubes with 1 tablespoon of olive oil and a pinch of salt and pepper.
    - Spread the cubes on a baking sheet in a single layer.
    - Roast for 20-25 minutes, or until tender and slightly caramelized, turning once halfway through. Set aside.
2. **Cook the Risotto:**
    - In a large skillet or saucepan, heat 1 tablespoon of olive oil over medium heat.
    - Add the chopped onion and cook until translucent, about 5 minutes.
    - Stir in the garlic and cook for another minute.
    - Add the sliced mushrooms and cook until they are softened and browned, about 5-7 minutes.
3. **Toast the Rice:**
    - Add the Arborio rice to the skillet and cook, stirring frequently, for about 2 minutes, until the rice is lightly toasted and coated with oil.
4. **Deglaze with Wine:**
    - Pour in the white wine and cook, stirring, until the wine is mostly absorbed by the rice.
5. **Add Broth Gradually:**
    - Begin adding the warm broth, one ladleful at a time, to the rice. Stir frequently and allow each addition to be absorbed before adding more. This process will take about 18-20 minutes.
    - Continue adding broth and stirring until the rice is creamy and cooked through but still al dente.
6. **Finish the Risotto:**

- Once the rice is cooked, gently fold in the roasted kabocha squash and the cooked mushrooms.
- Stir in the Parmesan cheese and butter, and season with salt and pepper to taste.
- Let the risotto sit for a couple of minutes to allow the flavors to meld.

7. **Serve:**
    - Garnish with fresh thyme or parsley if desired.
    - Serve the risotto warm, with extra Parmesan cheese on the side if you like.

Tips:

- For a richer flavor, you can use a combination of vegetable and chicken broth.
- If you prefer a creamier risotto, you can stir in a bit more butter or a splash of cream at the end.

Enjoy your creamy and satisfying kabocha and mushroom risotto!

Japanese Sweet Potato and Caramel Soup

Ingredients:

- 2 medium Japanese sweet potatoes (also known as satsumaimo), peeled and cubed
- 1 medium onion, chopped
- 2 cloves garlic, minced
- 1 tablespoon olive oil or unsalted butter
- 4 cups vegetable or chicken broth
- 1/2 cup heavy cream (optional, for a creamier texture)
- 2 tablespoons brown sugar
- 1 teaspoon sea salt (or to taste)
- 1/2 teaspoon black pepper (or to taste)
- 1/4 teaspoon ground cinnamon (optional)
- Fresh chives or parsley for garnish (optional)

Instructions:

1. **Prepare the Sweet Potatoes:**
   - Peel and cube the Japanese sweet potatoes.
2. **Cook the Sweet Potatoes:**
   - In a large pot, heat the olive oil or butter over medium heat.
   - Add the chopped onion and cook until translucent, about 5 minutes.
   - Stir in the minced garlic and cook for another minute until fragrant.
3. **Make the Caramel:**
   - In a small saucepan, melt the brown sugar over medium heat, stirring occasionally. Continue to cook until it turns into a deep amber caramel, but be careful not to let it burn.
   - Once the caramel is ready, carefully add a splash of broth to the pan. Stir to combine and dissolve the caramel. It will bubble up, so be cautious. Remove from heat.
4. **Combine Ingredients:**
   - Add the cubed sweet potatoes to the pot with the onions and garlic. Pour in the remaining broth and bring to a boil.
   - Reduce the heat and simmer until the sweet potatoes are tender, about 15-20 minutes.
5. **Blend the Soup:**
   - Once the sweet potatoes are tender, use an immersion blender to blend the soup until smooth. Alternatively, you can transfer the soup in batches to a blender.
6. **Add Caramel and Season:**
   - Stir in the caramel mixture into the blended soup. If using, add the heavy cream to make the soup richer and creamier.
   - Season with sea salt, black pepper, and ground cinnamon if desired. Adjust the seasoning to taste.
7. **Serve:**

- Ladle the soup into bowls and garnish with fresh chives or parsley if desired.

Tips:

- For a more complex flavor, you can add a pinch of nutmeg or a dash of cayenne pepper to the soup.
- If you prefer a less sweet soup, reduce the amount of caramel or brown sugar.

Enjoy your comforting and sweet Japanese sweet potato and caramel soup!

Teriyaki Tofu with Stir-Fried Greens

Ingredients:

For the Teriyaki Tofu:

- 1 block (14 ounces) firm or extra-firm tofu, drained and pressed
- 1/4 cup soy sauce
- 2 tablespoons mirin (or dry white wine as a substitute)
- 2 tablespoons sake (or dry white wine)
- 2 tablespoons brown sugar or honey
- 1 tablespoon grated fresh ginger
- 2 cloves garlic, minced
- 1 tablespoon cornstarch mixed with 2 tablespoons water (for thickening)
- 2 tablespoons vegetable oil (for cooking)

For the Stir-Fried Greens:

- 2 tablespoons vegetable oil
- 3 cups mixed greens (such as bok choy, spinach, kale, or Swiss chard), chopped
- 2 cloves garlic, minced
- 1 tablespoon soy sauce
- 1 teaspoon sesame oil
- 1 teaspoon sesame seeds (optional, for garnish)

Instructions:

1. **Prepare the Tofu:**
   - Slice the tofu into cubes or strips, depending on your preference.
   - In a medium bowl, mix the soy sauce, mirin, sake, brown sugar, grated ginger, and minced garlic to make the teriyaki sauce.
   - Add the tofu pieces to the bowl and gently toss to coat with the sauce. Marinate for at least 15 minutes, or up to 1 hour for more flavor.
2. **Cook the Tofu:**
   - Heat 2 tablespoons of vegetable oil in a large skillet or non-stick pan over medium-high heat.
   - Remove the tofu from the marinade, letting any excess drip off.
   - Add the tofu to the pan and cook until golden brown on all sides, about 5-7 minutes per side.
   - While the tofu is cooking, bring the remaining marinade to a simmer in a small saucepan. Add the cornstarch mixture and cook, stirring, until the sauce thickens.
   - Once the tofu is cooked, pour the thickened sauce over it and toss to coat. Cook for an additional 2-3 minutes until the tofu is well-glazed with the sauce.
3. **Prepare the Stir-Fried Greens:**

- In a separate large skillet or wok, heat 2 tablespoons of vegetable oil over medium-high heat.
- Add the minced garlic and cook for about 30 seconds until fragrant.
- Add the chopped greens and stir-fry for 3-5 minutes until they are wilted and tender.
- Add the soy sauce and sesame oil, and stir to combine. Cook for an additional minute.
- Garnish with sesame seeds if desired.

4. **Serve:**
   - Plate the teriyaki tofu alongside the stir-fried greens.
   - Serve with steamed rice or noodles if you like, and enjoy your meal!

Tips:

- Pressing the tofu is important to remove excess moisture, which helps it crisp up better during cooking.
- Feel free to customize the stir-fried greens with your favorites or what's in season.
- For added texture, you can sprinkle chopped green onions or toasted sesame seeds on top of the tofu.

This dish is both comforting and versatile, making it a great choice for a satisfying meal. Enjoy your teriyaki tofu with stir-fried greens!

Spicy Pumpkin Soup with Tofu

Ingredients:

For the Soup:

- 1 medium pumpkin (about 2-3 pounds), peeled, seeded, and cubed (or about 4 cups of canned pumpkin puree)
- 1 tablespoon olive oil
- 1 medium onion, chopped
- 2 cloves garlic, minced
- 1 tablespoon fresh ginger, minced
- 1-2 tablespoons curry powder (adjust to taste)
- 1 teaspoon ground cumin
- 1/2 teaspoon ground turmeric (optional)
- 1/4 teaspoon red pepper flakes (adjust to taste for spiciness)
- 4 cups vegetable or chicken broth
- 1 can (14 ounces) coconut milk
- Salt and pepper to taste
- 2 tablespoons lime juice or apple cider vinegar (optional, for added tanginess)

For the Tofu:

- 1 block (14 ounces) firm or extra-firm tofu, drained and pressed
- 2 tablespoons soy sauce
- 1 tablespoon olive oil
- 1 tablespoon cornstarch (optional, for extra crispiness)

Garnishes (optional):

- Fresh cilantro or parsley
- Pumpkin seeds
- A swirl of coconut milk
- Sliced red chilies

Instructions:

1. **Prepare the Tofu:**
   - Cut the tofu into cubes.
   - If desired, toss the tofu cubes with soy sauce and cornstarch for extra crispiness.
   - Heat 1 tablespoon of olive oil in a skillet over medium-high heat.
   - Add the tofu cubes and cook until golden and crispy on all sides, about 5-7 minutes. Remove from heat and set aside.
2. **Make the Soup:**
   - In a large pot, heat 1 tablespoon of olive oil over medium heat.
   - Add the chopped onion and cook until translucent, about 5 minutes.

- Stir in the minced garlic and ginger, and cook for another minute.
- Add the curry powder, ground cumin, turmeric (if using), and red pepper flakes. Stir for 1 minute until fragrant.
- Add the pumpkin cubes (or canned pumpkin puree) and pour in the vegetable or chicken broth. Bring to a boil.
- Reduce the heat and simmer until the pumpkin is tender, about 15-20 minutes if using fresh pumpkin.
- If using canned pumpkin puree, simmer for about 10 minutes to allow the flavors to meld.

3. **Blend the Soup:**
   - Use an immersion blender to blend the soup until smooth. Alternatively, carefully transfer the soup in batches to a blender and blend until smooth.
4. **Finish the Soup:**
   - Return the blended soup to the pot (if using a blender) and stir in the coconut milk. Heat through.
   - Season with salt and pepper to taste.
   - Add lime juice or apple cider vinegar if you like a bit of tanginess.
5. **Serve:**
   - Ladle the soup into bowls and top with the crispy tofu cubes.
   - Garnish with fresh cilantro or parsley, pumpkin seeds, a swirl of coconut milk, and sliced red chilies if desired.

Tips:

- Adjust the level of spiciness by varying the amount of red pepper flakes and curry powder.
- For added depth of flavor, you can roast the pumpkin cubes before adding them to the soup.
- If you prefer a less creamy soup, you can use light coconut milk or reduce the amount used.

Enjoy this flavorful and warming spicy pumpkin soup with tofu!

Japanese Salmon and Sweet Potato Bake

Ingredients:

- 4 salmon fillets (6 ounces each)
- 2 medium sweet potatoes, peeled and sliced into 1/4-inch rounds
- 2 tablespoons olive oil
- 3 tablespoons soy sauce
- 2 tablespoons mirin (or dry white wine as a substitute)
- 1 tablespoon sake (or dry white wine)
- 2 tablespoons brown sugar or honey
- 1 tablespoon grated fresh ginger
- 2 cloves garlic, minced
- 1 tablespoon sesame oil
- 2 teaspoons sesame seeds (optional, for garnish)
- 2 green onions, sliced (optional, for garnish)
- Salt and pepper to taste

Instructions:

1. **Prepare the Sweet Potatoes:**
   - Preheat your oven to 400°F (200°C).
   - Toss the sweet potato slices with olive oil, a pinch of salt, and pepper.
   - Spread the sweet potato slices in a single layer on a baking sheet or in a large baking dish.
2. **Bake the Sweet Potatoes:**
   - Roast the sweet potatoes in the preheated oven for about 20 minutes, or until they start to soften.
3. **Prepare the Salmon Marinade:**
   - In a small bowl, mix together the soy sauce, mirin, sake, brown sugar, grated ginger, and minced garlic.
4. **Marinate the Salmon:**
   - Pat the salmon fillets dry with paper towels and season lightly with salt and pepper.
   - Place the salmon fillets in a shallow dish and pour half of the marinade over them. Let the salmon marinate for at least 10 minutes, or up to 30 minutes for more flavor.
5. **Combine and Bake:**
   - After the sweet potatoes have been baking for 20 minutes, remove the baking sheet from the oven.
   - Arrange the marinated salmon fillets on top of the sweet potatoes.
   - Drizzle the remaining marinade over the salmon and sweet potatoes.
   - Return the baking sheet to the oven and bake for an additional 15-20 minutes, or until the salmon is cooked through and flakes easily with a fork, and the sweet potatoes are tender.

6. **Finish and Serve:**
    - Drizzle the baked salmon and sweet potatoes with sesame oil for extra flavor.
    - Garnish with sesame seeds and sliced green onions if desired.
    - Serve warm and enjoy!

Tips:

- For a bit of heat, you can add a dash of red pepper flakes to the marinade.
- If you prefer, you can add vegetables like bell peppers or snap peas to the baking dish for extra color and nutrition.
- Be sure not to overcook the salmon to keep it moist and tender.

This Japanese salmon and sweet potato bake is a delightful and healthy dish that's perfect for a weeknight dinner or a special occasion. Enjoy!

Miso Marinated Pumpkin Salad

Ingredients:

For the Miso Marinade:

- 2 tablespoons white miso paste
- 2 tablespoons rice vinegar
- 1 tablespoon soy sauce
- 1 tablespoon honey or maple syrup
- 1 tablespoon sesame oil
- 1 teaspoon grated fresh ginger
- 1 teaspoon minced garlic

For the Salad:

- 1 small pumpkin (such as kabocha or butternut), peeled, seeded, and cubed (about 4 cups)
- 2 tablespoons olive oil
- Salt and pepper to taste
- 2 cups mixed salad greens (e.g., arugula, spinach, or baby kale)
- 1/4 cup toasted pumpkin seeds
- 1/4 cup crumbled feta cheese or cubed avocado (optional, for extra richness)
- 2 green onions, thinly sliced (optional, for garnish)
- 1 tablespoon sesame seeds (optional, for garnish)

Instructions:

1. **Prepare the Miso Marinade:**
   - In a small bowl, whisk together the white miso paste, rice vinegar, soy sauce, honey or maple syrup, sesame oil, grated ginger, and minced garlic until smooth.
2. **Marinate the Pumpkin:**
   - Preheat your oven to 400°F (200°C).
   - Toss the cubed pumpkin with 1-2 tablespoons of the miso marinade, ensuring the pieces are well coated.
   - Spread the pumpkin cubes in a single layer on a baking sheet.
   - Roast in the oven for 20-25 minutes, or until the pumpkin is tender and slightly caramelized. Stir halfway through for even cooking.
3. **Assemble the Salad:**
   - While the pumpkin is roasting, prepare the salad greens and place them in a large bowl.
   - Once the pumpkin is done, let it cool slightly.
   - Toss the roasted pumpkin cubes with the remaining miso marinade (to taste) and add them to the salad greens.
4. **Add Toppings:**

- Sprinkle the salad with toasted pumpkin seeds, crumbled feta cheese or avocado, sliced green onions, and sesame seeds if using.
5. **Serve:**
    - Toss the salad gently to combine all the ingredients.
    - Serve immediately or chill for a refreshing cold salad.

Tips:

- If you prefer a different type of squash, such as butternut or acorn, you can substitute it in this recipe.
- For a more robust flavor, you can add a squeeze of fresh lime juice or a dash of red pepper flakes to the salad.
- The salad can be made ahead of time by roasting the pumpkin and storing it separately from the greens and toppings until ready to serve.

This miso marinated pumpkin salad is a delightful combination of sweet, savory, and umami flavors, making it a standout addition to any meal. Enjoy!

Grilled Eel with Autumn Vegetables

Ingredients:

For the Eel:

- 4 eel fillets (unagi), skin on
- 1/4 cup soy sauce
- 1/4 cup mirin (or dry white wine as a substitute)
- 1/4 cup sake (or dry white wine)
- 2 tablespoons sugar
- 1 clove garlic, minced
- 1 teaspoon fresh ginger, grated
- 1 tablespoon vegetable oil (for grilling)

For the Autumn Vegetables:

- 1 medium butternut squash, peeled, seeded, and cubed
- 1 cup Brussels sprouts, trimmed and halved
- 1 red bell pepper, sliced
- 1 medium red onion, sliced
- 2 tablespoons olive oil
- 1 teaspoon dried rosemary (or 1 tablespoon fresh rosemary leaves)
- 1 teaspoon dried thyme (or 1 tablespoon fresh thyme leaves)
- Salt and pepper to taste

Instructions:

1. **Prepare the Eel Glaze:**
    - In a small saucepan, combine the soy sauce, mirin, sake, sugar, minced garlic, and grated ginger.
    - Bring to a simmer over medium heat, stirring occasionally, until the sauce is slightly thickened and the sugar has dissolved. Remove from heat and let cool.
2. **Marinate the Eel:**
    - Place the eel fillets in a shallow dish and pour half of the cooled glaze over them.
    - Marinate the eel in the refrigerator for at least 30 minutes, or up to 2 hours for a more intense flavor.
3. **Prepare the Vegetables:**
    - Preheat your oven to 425°F (220°C).
    - Toss the butternut squash, Brussels sprouts, red bell pepper, and red onion with olive oil, dried rosemary, dried thyme, salt, and pepper.
    - Spread the vegetables in a single layer on a baking sheet.
    - Roast in the oven for about 25-30 minutes, or until the vegetables are tender and caramelized, stirring halfway through.
4. **Grill the Eel:**

- Preheat your grill to medium-high heat.
- Lightly brush the grill grates with vegetable oil to prevent sticking.
- Remove the eel from the marinade and place it on the grill.
- Grill the eel for about 3-4 minutes per side, or until cooked through and slightly charred. Brush with the remaining glaze during grilling for extra flavor.

5. **Serve:**
    - Arrange the grilled eel fillets on a serving platter.
    - Top with the roasted autumn vegetables.
    - Optionally, drizzle with any leftover glaze or garnish with fresh herbs.

Tips:

- If you don't have access to eel, you can substitute with other types of fish like salmon or tuna.
- For added flavor, you can sprinkle some sesame seeds or sliced green onions over the dish before serving.
- If you prefer, you can also serve this dish with a side of steamed rice or noodles.

This grilled eel with autumn vegetables is a wonderful way to enjoy seasonal produce with the rich, distinctive flavor of eel, making it a perfect dish for a special occasion or a cozy meal at home. Enjoy!

Sweet Potato and Walnut Rice Balls

Ingredients:

- 1 cup short-grain or sushi rice
- 1 1/4 cups water (for cooking rice)
- 1 medium sweet potato, peeled and cubed
- 1 tablespoon olive oil
- 1/4 cup walnuts, chopped
- 2 tablespoons soy sauce
- 1 tablespoon mirin (or dry white wine as a substitute)
- 1 teaspoon sesame oil
- Salt to taste
- Nori (seaweed) sheets, cut into strips or squares (optional, for wrapping)
- Sesame seeds for garnish (optional)

Instructions:

1. **Cook the Rice:**
   - Rinse the rice under cold water until the water runs clear.
   - Combine the rice and water in a rice cooker or saucepan.
   - Cook according to the rice cooker instructions or bring to a boil, then reduce heat to low, cover, and simmer for about 18 minutes. Let the rice sit for 10 minutes after cooking to firm up.
2. **Prepare the Sweet Potato:**
   - While the rice is cooking, place the sweet potato cubes in a pot and cover with water.
   - Bring to a boil, then reduce the heat and simmer until tender, about 10-15 minutes.
   - Drain the sweet potatoes and mash them with a fork or potato masher.
   - Heat olive oil in a skillet over medium heat.
   - Add the mashed sweet potatoes to the skillet and cook for about 3-4 minutes, stirring occasionally.
   - Stir in the soy sauce, mirin, and sesame oil. Cook for another 2-3 minutes until well combined and slightly thickened. Season with salt to taste.
3. **Combine Ingredients:**
   - Gently fold the chopped walnuts into the sweet potato mixture.
   - Combine the sweet potato mixture with the cooked rice. Mix well until evenly distributed.
4. **Shape the Rice Balls:**
   - Wet your hands to prevent sticking and take a small amount of the rice mixture.
   - Form it into a ball or triangle shape, pressing gently to compact it.
   - If using, wrap each rice ball with a strip or square of nori.
5. **Serve and Garnish:**
   - Optionally, sprinkle with sesame seeds before serving.

- Serve immediately or wrap in plastic wrap for later consumption.

Tips:

- You can adjust the amount of soy sauce and mirin according to your taste.
- For a more intense flavor, consider adding a bit of chopped scallions or a pinch of ground ginger to the sweet potato mixture.
- These rice balls can be enjoyed warm or at room temperature, making them versatile for various occasions.

Enjoy your sweet potato and walnut rice balls as a delicious and satisfying snack or meal!

Hot Pot with Kabocha and Tofu

Ingredients:

For the Broth:

- 6 cups dashi stock (or chicken/vegetable broth)
- 1/4 cup soy sauce
- 2 tablespoons mirin
- 1 tablespoon sake (or dry white wine as a substitute)
- 1 tablespoon sugar (optional, adjust to taste)
- 1 piece kombu (dried kelp), about 4 inches (optional, for added umami)

For the Hot Pot:

- 1 small kabocha squash, peeled, seeded, and cut into bite-sized cubes
- 1 block (14 ounces) firm or extra-firm tofu, drained and cut into cubes
- 1 cup shiitake or cremini mushrooms, sliced
- 1 cup napa cabbage or bok choy, chopped
- 1 carrot, peeled and sliced
- 1 cup spinach or other leafy greens
- 2-3 green onions, sliced
- 1-2 garlic cloves, minced
- 1 teaspoon grated fresh ginger
- 2 tablespoons vegetable oil

Optional Add-Ins:

- Udon noodles or rice noodles
- Thinly sliced beef or chicken (if desired)
- Soy sauce, sesame oil, and/or chili sauce for dipping

Instructions:

1. **Prepare the Broth:**
   - In a large pot or hot pot, combine the dashi stock (or broth), soy sauce, mirin, sake, and sugar (if using).
   - If using kombu, add it to the pot and bring to a simmer over medium heat. Remove the kombu before the broth reaches a boil.
   - Let the broth simmer for about 5-10 minutes to allow the flavors to meld. Adjust seasoning as needed.
2. **Prepare the Ingredients:**
   - Heat vegetable oil in a large skillet over medium heat.
   - Add the minced garlic and grated ginger, and cook for about 1 minute until fragrant.

- Add the sliced mushrooms and cook for 3-4 minutes until they start to soften. Remove from heat and set aside.
3. **Cook the Hot Pot:**
    - Add the kabocha squash and carrot to the simmering broth and cook for about 10-15 minutes, or until the vegetables are tender.
    - Gently add the tofu cubes to the pot and cook for an additional 5-7 minutes.
    - Add the napa cabbage or bok choy and cook for another 3-5 minutes until the greens are wilted.
4. **Add Optional Ingredients:**
    - If using noodles or additional proteins, add them to the pot according to their cooking times. For example, if using udon noodles, add them in the last 5 minutes of cooking.
5. **Serve:**
    - Ladle the hot pot into individual bowls, making sure to include a variety of vegetables and tofu in each serving.
    - Garnish with sliced green onions and any other optional garnishes you like.
    - Serve with additional dipping sauces or condiments, such as soy sauce, sesame oil, or chili sauce, if desired.

Tips:

- Feel free to customize the hot pot with your favorite vegetables or mushrooms.
- For added flavor, you can include a splash of rice vinegar or a sprinkle of sesame seeds before serving.
- This dish is perfect for sharing with family or friends; simply place the hot pot at the center of the table and let everyone serve themselves.

Enjoy your delicious and comforting hot pot with kabocha and tofu!

Udon with Sweet Potato and Spinach

Ingredients:

For the Udon:

- 12 ounces fresh or frozen udon noodles
- 1 medium sweet potato, peeled and cubed
- 1 tablespoon olive oil
- 2 cups fresh spinach
- 2 cloves garlic, minced
- 1 tablespoon fresh ginger, minced
- 2 tablespoons soy sauce
- 1 tablespoon mirin (or dry white wine as a substitute)
- 1 tablespoon sesame oil
- 1 tablespoon sesame seeds (optional, for garnish)
- 2 green onions, sliced (optional, for garnish)

Optional Add-Ins:

- 1 cup sliced mushrooms (such as shiitake or cremini)
- 1 cup thinly sliced carrots
- 1 tablespoon hoisin sauce or miso paste (for extra flavor)
- Chili flakes or sriracha (for a spicy kick)

Instructions:

1. **Prepare the Sweet Potato:**
    - Preheat your oven to 425°F (220°C).
    - Toss the sweet potato cubes with olive oil, salt, and pepper.
    - Spread the sweet potato cubes on a baking sheet in a single layer.
    - Roast for 20-25 minutes, or until tender and caramelized, stirring halfway through. Set aside.
2. **Cook the Udon Noodles:**
    - If using fresh udon noodles, bring a pot of water to a boil. Add the noodles and cook according to the package instructions, usually for about 2-3 minutes. Drain and set aside.
    - If using frozen udon noodles, follow the package instructions for cooking and then drain.
3. **Prepare the Stir-Fry (or Broth):**
    - Heat sesame oil in a large skillet or wok over medium heat.
    - Add the minced garlic and ginger, and sauté for about 1 minute until fragrant.
    - If using, add sliced mushrooms and carrots and stir-fry for about 3-4 minutes until tender.

- Add the roasted sweet potatoes and cook for an additional 2 minutes, stirring gently.
- Add the spinach and cook until wilted, about 1 minute.

4. **Combine and Season:**
   - Add the cooked udon noodles to the skillet or wok.
   - Pour in the soy sauce and mirin, and toss everything together until well combined and heated through.
   - If desired, stir in hoisin sauce or miso paste for extra flavor.

5. **Serve:**
   - Divide the udon mixture among serving bowls.
   - Garnish with sesame seeds and sliced green onions if desired.
   - For a spicy kick, drizzle with a bit of sriracha or sprinkle with chili flakes.

Tips:

- You can adjust the seasoning to taste by adding more soy sauce or a dash of rice vinegar if you like.
- For added protein, consider including tofu or cooked chicken.
- This dish can be served hot or at room temperature, making it versatile for different occasions.

Enjoy your flavorful and comforting udon with sweet potato and spinach!

Japanese Style Squash and Apple Soup

Ingredients:

- 1 medium butternut squash (or kabocha squash), peeled, seeded, and cubed (about 4 cups)
- 1 medium apple (such as Fuji or Honeycrisp), peeled, cored, and chopped
- 1 medium onion, chopped
- 2 cloves garlic, minced
- 1 tablespoon fresh ginger, minced
- 4 cups vegetable or chicken broth
- 1/2 cup coconut milk (or heavy cream for a richer soup)
- 2 tablespoons soy sauce
- 1 tablespoon mirin (or dry white wine as a substitute)
- 1 tablespoon sesame oil
- Salt and pepper to taste
- 1 tablespoon sesame seeds (optional, for garnish)
- 2 green onions, sliced (optional, for garnish)
- Fresh cilantro or parsley (optional, for garnish)

Instructions:

1. **Prepare the Ingredients:**
    - Heat sesame oil in a large pot over medium heat.
    - Add the chopped onion and cook until translucent, about 5 minutes.
    - Stir in the minced garlic and ginger, and cook for another minute until fragrant.
2. **Cook the Squash and Apple:**
    - Add the cubed squash and chopped apple to the pot.
    - Pour in the vegetable or chicken broth and bring to a boil.
    - Reduce the heat to low and simmer until the squash and apple are tender, about 20-25 minutes.
3. **Blend the Soup:**
    - Use an immersion blender to blend the soup until smooth. Alternatively, carefully transfer the soup in batches to a blender and blend until smooth.
4. **Add Creaminess and Seasoning:**
    - Return the blended soup to the pot (if using a blender).
    - Stir in the coconut milk (or heavy cream) and add soy sauce and mirin.
    - Heat through, stirring occasionally. Adjust seasoning with salt and pepper to taste.
5. **Serve:**
    - Ladle the soup into bowls.
    - Garnish with sesame seeds, sliced green onions, and fresh cilantro or parsley if desired.

Tips:

- For a bit of heat, you can add a pinch of red pepper flakes or a small amount of finely chopped chili.
- If you prefer a thicker soup, reduce the amount of broth or increase the amount of squash.
- For added texture, you can top the soup with a swirl of coconut milk or a few toasted pumpkin seeds.

This Japanese-style squash and apple soup is a delightful blend of sweet and savory flavors, perfect for warming up on a cool day. Enjoy!

Roasted Mushroom and Pork Stir-Fry

Ingredients:

For the Roasted Mushrooms:

- 8 ounces (about 2 cups) mushrooms (such as cremini, shiitake, or button), cleaned and sliced
- 2 tablespoons olive oil
- 1 teaspoon dried thyme or rosemary (optional)
- Salt and pepper to taste

For the Pork Stir-Fry:

- 1 pound pork tenderloin or pork shoulder, thinly sliced (about 1/4-inch thick)
- 2 tablespoons vegetable oil
- 1 bell pepper, sliced
- 1 medium onion, sliced
- 2 cloves garlic, minced
- 1 tablespoon fresh ginger, minced
- 2 tablespoons soy sauce
- 2 tablespoons hoisin sauce
- 1 tablespoon rice vinegar
- 1 tablespoon oyster sauce (optional)
- 1 teaspoon cornstarch mixed with 2 tablespoons water (for thickening, optional)
- 2 green onions, sliced (for garnish)
- Sesame seeds (for garnish, optional)

Instructions:

1. **Roast the Mushrooms:**
    - Preheat your oven to 425°F (220°C).
    - Toss the sliced mushrooms with olive oil, dried thyme or rosemary (if using), salt, and pepper.
    - Spread the mushrooms in a single layer on a baking sheet.
    - Roast for 15-20 minutes, or until the mushrooms are golden brown and tender, stirring halfway through.
2. **Prepare the Pork:**
    - While the mushrooms are roasting, heat vegetable oil in a large skillet or wok over medium-high heat.
    - Add the sliced pork and cook until browned and cooked through, about 5-7 minutes. Remove the pork from the skillet and set aside.
3. **Stir-Fry the Vegetables:**
    - In the same skillet, add a little more oil if needed.

- Add the sliced bell pepper and onion. Stir-fry for about 3-4 minutes until they start to soften.
        - Add the minced garlic and ginger, and stir-fry for another minute until fragrant.
4. **Combine and Sauce:**
    - Return the cooked pork to the skillet with the vegetables.
    - Add the roasted mushrooms to the skillet.
    - Pour in the soy sauce, hoisin sauce, rice vinegar, and oyster sauce (if using). Stir to coat everything evenly.
    - If you want a thicker sauce, stir in the cornstarch mixture and cook for an additional 1-2 minutes until the sauce has thickened.
5. **Garnish and Serve:**
    - Garnish with sliced green onions and sesame seeds if desired.
    - Serve hot over steamed rice or noodles.

Tips:

- For extra flavor, you can add a pinch of red pepper flakes or a splash of chili sauce if you like a bit of heat.
- Feel free to include additional vegetables such as snap peas, broccoli, or carrots for a more colorful and nutritious dish.
- If you prefer a lighter version, you can use a low-sodium soy sauce and skip the oyster sauce.

This roasted mushroom and pork stir-fry is a rich and satisfying dish with a delightful mix of textures and flavors. Enjoy!

Pumpkin and Ginger Muffins

Ingredients:

- 1 1/2 cups all-purpose flour
- 1/2 teaspoon baking powder
- 1 teaspoon baking soda
- 1 teaspoon ground cinnamon
- 1/2 teaspoon ground ginger
- 1/4 teaspoon ground cloves
- 1/2 teaspoon salt
- 1/2 cup granulated sugar
- 1/4 cup brown sugar, packed
- 1/2 cup vegetable oil
- 1 cup canned pumpkin (not pumpkin pie filling)
- 2 large eggs
- 1/4 cup plain Greek yogurt or sour cream
- 1 teaspoon vanilla extract
- 1 tablespoon grated fresh ginger (optional, for extra zing)
- 1/2 cup chopped walnuts or pecans (optional, for added crunch)

For the Topping (Optional):

- 2 tablespoons granulated sugar
- 1/2 teaspoon ground cinnamon

Instructions:

1. **Preheat the Oven:**
   - Preheat your oven to 350°F (175°C).
   - Line a muffin tin with paper liners or lightly grease it.
2. **Mix Dry Ingredients:**
   - In a medium bowl, whisk together the flour, baking powder, baking soda, cinnamon, ground ginger, ground cloves, and salt.
3. **Mix Wet Ingredients:**
   - In a large bowl, whisk together the granulated sugar, brown sugar, and vegetable oil until well combined.
   - Add the pumpkin, eggs, Greek yogurt (or sour cream), and vanilla extract. Mix until smooth.
   - If using, stir in the grated fresh ginger.
4. **Combine Wet and Dry Ingredients:**
   - Gently fold the dry ingredients into the wet ingredients until just combined. Be careful not to overmix.
   - If using, fold in the chopped nuts.
5. **Prepare the Muffin Tin:**

- Divide the batter evenly among the muffin cups, filling each about 3/4 full.
6. **Add Topping (Optional):**
    - In a small bowl, mix the granulated sugar with ground cinnamon.
    - Sprinkle a little of this mixture on top of each muffin for a sweet, spiced crust.
7. **Bake:**
    - Bake in the preheated oven for 20-25 minutes, or until a toothpick inserted into the center comes out clean.
8. **Cool:**
    - Allow the muffins to cool in the tin for 5 minutes, then transfer them to a wire rack to cool completely.

Tips:

- For a more intense ginger flavor, you can increase the amount of ground ginger or fresh grated ginger.
- You can substitute half of the all-purpose flour with whole wheat flour for a slightly healthier version.
- These muffins freeze well, so you can make a batch ahead of time and store them in an airtight container or freezer bag.

Enjoy these delicious pumpkin and ginger muffins with a cup of tea or coffee for a cozy treat!

Soy-Glazed Chicken Wings with Roasted Fall Veggies

Ingredients:

For the Soy-Glazed Chicken Wings:

- 2 pounds chicken wings
- 1/4 cup soy sauce
- 1/4 cup honey or maple syrup
- 2 tablespoons rice vinegar
- 2 tablespoons hoisin sauce
- 1 tablespoon sesame oil
- 2 cloves garlic, minced
- 1 tablespoon fresh ginger, minced
- 1 teaspoon cornstarch (optional, for thickening)

For the Roasted Fall Veggies:

- 1 medium butternut squash, peeled, seeded, and cubed
- 2 carrots, peeled and sliced
- 1 red bell pepper, sliced
- 1 red onion, cut into wedges
- 2 tablespoons olive oil
- 1 teaspoon dried thyme
- 1 teaspoon dried rosemary
- Salt and pepper to taste

Instructions:

1. **Prepare the Soy Glaze:**
    - In a medium bowl, whisk together the soy sauce, honey or maple syrup, rice vinegar, hoisin sauce, sesame oil, minced garlic, and minced ginger.
    - If you prefer a thicker glaze, dissolve the cornstarch in a little water and whisk it into the sauce. Set aside.
2. **Marinate the Chicken Wings:**
    - Place the chicken wings in a large bowl or zip-top bag.
    - Pour half of the soy glaze over the wings and toss to coat evenly.
    - Marinate in the refrigerator for at least 30 minutes, or up to 4 hours for more flavor.
3. **Roast the Fall Veggies:**
    - Preheat your oven to 425°F (220°C).
    - In a large bowl, toss the butternut squash, carrots, red bell pepper, and red onion with olive oil, dried thyme, dried rosemary, salt, and pepper.
    - Spread the vegetables in a single layer on a baking sheet.

- Roast for 25-30 minutes, or until the vegetables are tender and caramelized, stirring halfway through.
4. **Cook the Chicken Wings:**
   - Preheat your grill to medium-high heat or preheat your oven to 400°F (200°C) if baking.
   - Remove the chicken wings from the marinade, shaking off excess.
   - **For Grilling:** Grill the wings for about 8-10 minutes per side, or until fully cooked and crispy, basting with the remaining glaze during the last few minutes of grilling.
   - **For Baking:** Arrange the wings in a single layer on a baking sheet lined with foil or parchment paper. Bake for 30-35 minutes, flipping halfway through, until crispy and cooked through. Brush with the remaining glaze during the last 10 minutes of baking.
5. **Serve:**
   - Arrange the soy-glazed chicken wings on a serving platter.
   - Serve alongside the roasted fall vegetables.
   - Optionally, garnish with sesame seeds or chopped green onions for extra flavor.

Tips:

- For added flavor, you can sprinkle the wings with sesame seeds or chopped fresh cilantro before serving.
- If you like your wings extra crispy, you can broil them for a few minutes at the end of baking or grilling.
- Feel free to adjust the amount of honey or maple syrup in the glaze based on your sweetness preference.

This soy-glazed chicken wings with roasted fall veggies recipe is a perfect balance of savory, sweet, and comforting flavors. Enjoy!